Audi
Vorsprung durch Technik

G000139238

A
A
D

Art Architecture Design

BERLIN

edited by Martin Nicholas Kunz + Lizzy Courage

teNeues

Intro ART	8	Contemporary Fine Arts	24	Neue Nationalgalerie	
Seven Star Gallery	10	Museum The Kennedys	26	Hamburger Bahnhof –	
Me Collectors Room Berlin	12	Galerie Thomas Schulte	28	Museum für Gegenwart [	
KW Institute of Contemporary Art	14	Galerie Ulrich Fiedler	30	Helmut Newton Stiftun	
C/O Berlin	16	East Side Gallery	32	im Museum für Fotogra	
Sammlung Boros	18	Berlinische Galerie	36	Camera Work	
Portrait – Boros	22	Martin-Gropius-Bau	40	Haus am Waldsee	

Intro ARCHITECTURE	58	Mini Loft	76	E-Werk	
Aedes am Pfefferberg	60	Band des Bundes	78	Portrait – HSH	
Neues Museum	62	Akademie der Künste	82	Topographie des Terrors	
Jacob-und-Wilhelm-Grimm-Zentrum	66	Denkmal für die ermordeten		Jüdisches Museum Berlir	
Collegium Hungaricum Berlin	68	Juden Europas	84	Bauhaus-Archiv Berlin	
Deutsches Historisches Museum	70	Science Center		Liquidrom	
Niederländische Botschaft	72	Medizintechnik	86	Philologische Bibliothek	
Hochschule für Musik Hanns Eisler	74				

Intro DESIGN	110	Oliv	128	Schönhauser Design	
Ackselhaus & Blue Home	112	Tadshikische Teestube	130	Buchhandlung Walther Kön	
Soho House Berlin	114	Cha Chà Positive Eating	132	Quartier 206	
Hotel AMANO	116	Birgit von Heintze Interiors	134	Exil Wohnmagazin	
Cosmo Hotel Berlin	118	Lunettes Selection	136	Bücherbogen Savignyplatz	
Hotel Michelberger	120	Dandy of the Grotesque	138	Villa Harteneck	
Portrait – Werner Aisslinger	124	Salon Bennett	140	Kino International	
Themroc	126				

| Map | 158 | Service | 160 | Credits // Imprint | |

ART
ARCHITECTURE
DESIGN
BERLIN

A
A
D

Content

Any traveler to the German capital quickly notices that Berlin is hard to compare with any other major metropolis: ultramodern architecture next to registered historical monuments, chic boutiques and bars right next-door to corner pubs, parties being held in dilapidated old buildings repurposed as dance clubs. Berlin style is a quirky aesthetic of the unglamorous, a new form of German understatement with a confident cosmopolitanism projected by the city. This unique atmosphere attracts creative individuals and art lovers from all over the world, who flock to live and work in this city on the banks of the Spree—or just to enjoy its diversity. Influences from a wide variety of cultures and styles intermingle with German history to form an eclectic mélange found only in Berlin. The omnipresent past meets the spirit of change. Artists, architects and designers of national and international stature come together, collectively fashioning the Berlin of the future.

Jeder, der die deutsche Hauptstadt bereist, merkt schnell, dass Berlin mit keiner anderen Weltstadt zu vergleichen ist. Modernste Architektur trifft auf Baudenkmäler, trendige Shops und Bars eröffnen direkt neben alten Eckkneipen, man feiert Partys in runtergekommenen Altbauten, zum Club umfunktioniert. Eine ganz eigene Ästhetik des Unglamourösen macht den Berlin-Stil zu einer neuen Form von deutschem Understatement, und Berlin präsentiert sich bewusst kosmopolitisch. Die einzigartige Atmosphäre lockt Kreative und Kunstliebhaber aus aller Welt in die Stadt an der Spree um hier zu leben, zu arbeiten oder einfach nur die vielfältige Kulturszene zu genießen. Einflüsse unterschiedlichster Kulturen und Stile vermischen sich mit deutscher Geschichte zu einem eklektischen Mix, wie man ihn nur in Berlin findet. Die allgegenwärtige Vergangenheit trifft auf den Esprit der Veränderung. In diesem Spannungsfeld treffen sich nationale und internationale Künstler, Architekten und Designer und gestalten gemeinsam das zukünftige Berlin.

Quiconque flâne dans la capitale allemande s'aperçoit très vite qu'aucune autre grande ville de renommée mondiale ne peut être comparée avec Berlin. Une architecture des plus modernes côtoie des monuments historiques, boutiques et bars branchés ouvrent leurs portes à deux pas d'anciens troquets, des soirées sont organisées dans des bâtiments délabrés faisant office pour l'occasion de clubs. Une interprétation esthétique toute personnelle de l'anti-glamour confère au style berlinois une forme nouvelle d'understatement à l'allemande et fait de Berlin une destination cosmopolite incontournable. L'atmosphère unique de cette ville attire esprits créatifs et amateurs d'art des quatre coins du globe sur les rives de la Spree, où il fait bon vivre, travailler ou tout simplement s'imprégner de la diversité du paysage culturel. Styles et cultures les plus divers fusionnent avec l'histoire allemande, créant un mélange éclectique propre à Berlin. Le passé omniprésent cohabite avec l'esprit du changement. Au cœur des tensions engendrées par des mutations, artistes, architectes et créateurs tant nationaux qu'internationaux se donnent rendez-vous pour façonner ensemble le futur Berlin.

Quienes visitan la capital alemana comprueban pronto que Berlín no puede compararse a ninguna otra gran ciudad del mundo. La arquitectura más moderna convive con edificios protegidos, las tiendas de vanguardia y los locales nocturnos comparten calle con bares de los de toda la vida, se organizan fiestas en decrépitos edificios reconvertidos en discotecas. Una estética propia, voluntariamente alejada de todo glamour, hace del estilo berlinés una nueva forma de understatement alemán, a través del cual Berlín erige su imagen conscientemente cosmopolita. Su incomparable ambiente atrae a mentes creadoras y amantes del arte de todo el mundo para vivir, trabajar y o simplemente disfrutar de la inmensa oferta cultural a orillas del Spree. Los influjos de las más diversas culturas y estilos se entremezclan con la historia alemana para desembocar en un todo ecléctico que sólo existe en Berlín. La omnipresencia del pasado cohabita con el espíritu del cambio, y en esta dialéctica trabajan artistas, arquitectos y diseñadores de renombre nacional e internacional para dar cara al Berlín del futuro.

ART

A

A few years ago, no one would have thought to call Berlin an art center. Rich museum collections and artist enclaves in the Eastern and Western sectors notwithstanding, it was not until the 1990s that the art scene experienced an enduring revival when projects like Kunsthaus Tacheles and C/O Berlin developed into art production and presentation spaces. Artists from all over the world found inspiration and affordable studios in Berlin, then collectors and dealers followed. Former refugees like Heinz Berggruen and Helmut Newton willed their works to the city of their birth, and private collections like those of Erich Marx and Christian Boros enriched the city with new art locales. German and international galleries opened branches or moved their entire operations to the German capital, which now boasts the highest density of galleries in Europe. With them, Berlin established itself as a brand in the booming market for contemporary art, celebrated in spectacular events like Gallery Weekend or the Berlin Biennale.

Niemandem wäre noch vor ein paar Jahren eingefallen, Berlin als Kunstmetropole zu bezeichnen. Trotz reich gefüllter Museen und Künstlerenklaven in Ost und West erlebte die Kunstszene erst in den 1990er Jahren einen andauernden Aufschwung, als sich Initiativen wie das Kunsthaus Tacheles oder C/O Berlin zu Produktions- und Präsentationsräumen für Kunst entwickelten. Künstler aus aller Welt fanden in Berlin Inspiration und erschwingliche Ateliers. Den Künstlern folgten die Sammler und Händler. Ehemalige Flüchtlinge wie Heinz Berggruen und Helmut Newton vermachten ihrer Geburtsstadt ihre Werke, und private Sammlungen wie die von Erich Marx und Christian Boros bescherten der Stadt neue Kunstorte. Deutsche und internationale Galerien eröffnen Dependancen oder ziehen gleich ganz in die deutsche Hauptstadt, die inzwischen die höchste Galeriendichte in Europa aufweist. Mit ihnen etablierte sich Berliner Kunst als Marke auf dem boomenden Markt für zeitgenössische Kunst, die sich in Spektakeln wie dem Gallery Weekend oder der Berlin Biennale zelebriert.

Il y a encore quelques années, il ne serait venu à l'esprit de personne que Berlin serait un jour qualifié de métropole artistique. Malgré la présence de musées fourmillant d'œuvres et d'enclaves d'artistes à l'Est comme à l'Ouest, la scène artistique berlinoise a connu un essor constant seulement dans les années 1990, lorsque des associations telles que le Kunsthaus Tacheles ou le C/O Berlin transformèrent leurs locaux en ateliers de travail et galeries d'exposition. Des artistes de tout horizon trouvèrent à Berlin l'inspiration mais aussi des ateliers à des prix abordables. Collectionneurs et marchands succédèrent ensuite aux artistes. D'anciens réfugiés comme Heinz Berggruen et Helmut Newton léguèrent leurs œuvres à leur ville natale, tandis que des collections privées, par exemple celle d'Erich Marx et de Christian Boros, ont permis à la ville de s'enrichir de nouveaux espaces consacrés à l'art. Des galeries allemandes et internationales inaugurèrent des succursales ou s'installèrent tout bonnement dans la capitale, qui entre-temps recense la plus forte « densité » de galeries d'art en Europe. Sans oublier l'art berlinois qui a su s'établir comme marque sur le marché de l'art contemporain en pleine expansion, auquel il est rendu hommage lors de grands événements culturels tels que le Gallery Weekend ou la Berlin Biennale.

No hace demasiado tiempo, a nadie se le habría ocurrido hablar de Berlín como capital de las artes. Pese a sus bien dotados museos y a los enclaves artísticos en en el Este y el Oeste de la ciudad, hubo que esperar a la década de 1990 para que las artes recibiesen un impulso duradero, cuando las iniciativas como Kunsthaus Tacheles o C/O Berlin se materializaron en espacios de producción y exposición. Artistas de todo el mundo encontraron inspiración y talleres asequibles en Berlín, y a su estela llegaron los coleccionistas y marchantes. Berlineses emigrados como Heinz Berggruen y Helmut Newton legaron su obra a su ciudad natal, y las colecciones privadas (como las de Erich Marx y Christian Boros) la dotaron de nuevos espacios artísticos. Galerías alemanas e internacionales abrieron locales o se trasladaron por completo a la capital reunificada, que cuenta ahora con la mayor densidad de galerías en toda Europa. A través de ellas, el arte berlinés se ha establecido como una marca en el creciente mercado del arte contemporáneo, que encuentra su máxima expresión en espectáculos como el Gallery Weekend o la Berlin Biennale.

SEVEN STAR GALLERY

Gormannstraße 7 // Mitte
Tel.: +49 (0)30 84 71 18 77
www.sevenstargallery.com

Tue–Sat 1 pm to 8 pm
U8 Weinmeisterstraße

Unlike galleries that present objects in white cubes, Seven Star Gallery shows works of photography in completely unrenovated rooms oozing the charm of a Berlin apartment from the 1930s. Large-format prints are displayed against exposed brick walls and rough plaster—some of them limited editions of previously unpublished works by international art photographers. Changing exhibitions show works by Joachim Baldorf, Will McBride and Donata Wensers.

Anders als Galerien, die Objekte in reinweißen Ausstellungsräumen präsentieren, zeigt die Seven Star Galerie Fotografie in gänzlich unsanierten Räumen, die den Charme einer Berliner Wohnung aus den 1930er Jahren verströmen. Auf freigelegten Backsteinwänden und Rauputz sind die großformatigen Abzüge gehängt – teilweise limitierte Auflagen bisher unveröffentlichter Werke internationaler Fotokünstler. Wechselnde Ausstellungen zeigen unter anderem Arbeiten von Joachim Baldorf, Will McBride und Donata Wensers.

Contrastant avec les galeries aux murs et aux supports blancs, la galerie Seven Star présente des œuvres de photographie dans des pièces non rénovées, qui reflètent le charme des habitations berlinoises des années 30. Des clichés y sont exposés aux murs de briques crépis, dont certains sont des œuvres de photographes célèbres qui n'ont encore jamais été rendues publiques. Les travaux d'artistes tels que Joachim Baldorf, Will McBride, et Donata Wensers y sont présentés lors d'expositions temporaires.

A diferencia de otras galerías en las que las piezas se exponen en prístinas salas blancas, la Seven Star Galerie presenta la fotografía en espacios sin renovar, que irradian todo el encanto de las viviendas berlinesas de los años treinta. Las imágenes (en parte copias limitadas e inéditas de eminentes fotógrafos internacionales) se muestran sobre paredes de ladrillo desnudo o apenas revocadas. Sus numerosas exposiciones han mostrado obras, entre otros, de Joachim Baldorf, Will McBride y Donata Wensers.

Thomas Olbricht, too, relocated to the German capital with most of his collection of 2,500 works by Old Masters and contemporary artists. He designed the 35,800-sq.-ft. residential and exhibition building with Düttmann + Kleymann architects. The Olbricht Collection shows the themes of eros, death and vanitas from constantly new aspects in three exhibits each year. It is complemented by the Wunderkammer, a miscellany of antique items.

Auch Thomas Olbricht hat sich mit einem Großteil seiner 2 500 Werke umfassenden Sammlung Alter Meister und zeitgenössischer Kunst in der deutschen Hauptstadt niedergelassen. Er konzipiert das 3 330 m² große Wohn- und Ausstellungsgebäude zusammen mit dem Architekturbüro Düttmann + Kleymann. In jährlich drei Ausstellungen zeigt die Olbricht Collection die Themen Eros, Tod und Vanitas aus immer neuen Blickwinkeln. Sie wird durch die „Wunderkammer" ergänzt, einem Sammelsurium antiker Gegenstände.

Thomas Olbricht s'est également installé, avec une grande partie de sa collection de 2 500 œuvres des grands maîtres et d'art contemporain, dans la capitale allemande. Il conçut cet immeuble d'habitations et d'expositions d'une surface de 3 330 m² avec les architectes Düttmann + Kleymann. A l'occasion de trois expositions annuelles, la collection expose des œuvres traitant de diverses thématiques comme l'éros, la mort et la vanité en les présentant sous un nouvel angle. La « caverne aux merveilles » abrite un bric-à-brac d'antiquités.

Thomas Olbricht se ha instalado en la capital alemana con buena parte de su colección, unas 2 500 obras de arte clásico y contemporáneo. El fue quien, con la colaboración del despacho de arquitectos Düttmann + Kleymann, concibió el edificio de 3 330 m², a un tiempo residencia y sala de exposiciones. En el marco de las tres exposiciones anuales, la colección aborda los temas de Eros, Thanatos y Vanitas desde perspectivas siempre novedosas. El "gabinete de las maravillas", un abigarrado conjunto de antigüedades, complementa la colección.

ME COLLECTORS ROOM BERLIN

Auguststraße 68 // Mitte
Tel.: +49 (0)30 86 00 85 10
www.me-berlin.com

Tue–Sun noon to 6 pm
U6 Oranienburger Tor, U8 Weinmeisterstraße,
S1, S2, S25 Oranienburger Straße

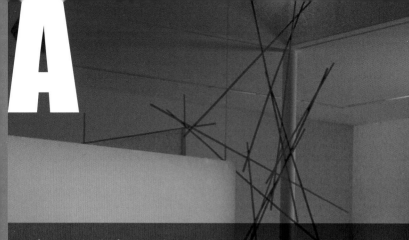

A former margarine factory in the heart of Berlin's Scheunenviertel provides ample space for one of the leading institutions for contemporary art. The KW Institute for Contemporary Art, often referred to as KW, does not have a collection of its own. Instead, KW provides 22,000 sq. ft. of exhibition space, artist studios, and a café located in a spacious courtyard in a multifaceted effort to support innovation, creative work and cultural exchange. KW launched the Berlin Biennale for Contemporary Art in 1996.

Eine ehemalige Margarinefabrik inmitten des Berliner Scheunenviertels bietet Raum für eine der führenden Institutionen für zeitgenössische Kunst. Das KW Institute for Contemporary Art, auch KW genannt, verfügt über keine eigene Sammlung; eine Ausstellungsfläche von 2000 m², Künstlerstudios und ein großzügiger Innenhof mit Café lassen Freiraum für Innovation, kreative Arbeit und kulturellen Austausch. 1996 war hier die Geburtstätte der Berlin Biennale für zeitgenössische Kunst.

Une ancienne usine de margarine, au cœur du quartier Scheunenviertel à Berlin, abrite l'une des principales institutions d'art contemporain de la capitale. Le centre d'art contemporain, le Kunstwerke, ne possède pas sa propre collection d'art. 2000 m² de surface d'exposition, des ateliers et une vaste cour intérieure avec un café, en font un lieu favorisant l'innovation artistique, le travail créatif et l'échange culturel. C'est ici qu'est née l'exposition d'art contemporain, la Berlin Biennale, en 1996.

Una antigua fábrica de margarina en pleno Scheunenviertel ofrece espacio para una de las instituciones más importantes de arte contemporáneo. El KW Institute for Contemporary Art, también llamado KW, no dispone de una colección propia; una superficie de exposición de 2000 m², estudios de arte y un amplio patio con café crean un espacio libre para la innovación, el trabajo creativo y el intercambio cultural. Aquí nació en 1996 la Berlin Biennale para arte contemporáneo.

KW INSTITUTE
OF CONTEMPORARY ART

Auguststraße 69 // Mitte
Tel.: +49 (0)30 2 43 45 90
www.kw-berlin.de

Tue–Sun noon to 7 pm, Thu noon to 9 pm
U6 Oranienburger Tor, U8 Weinmeisterstraße,
S1, S2, S25 Oranienburger Straße

C/O BERLIN

Oranienburger Straße 35–36 // Mitte
Tel.: +49 (0)30 28 09 19 25
www.co-berlin.info

Daily 11 am to 8 pm
U6 Oranienburger Tor, S1, S2, S25 Oranienburger Straße

Since 2000, the privately funded International Forum For Visual Dialogues has regularly hosted temporary exhibitions of various well-known contemporary photographers. The venerable Royal Post Office building, remodeled in 2006 by architect and co-founder Ingo Pott, houses the works of grand masters, and is likewise a forum for lectures and discussions with the artists. C/O Berlin will continue this programme of events, though it will be obliged to relocate in 2011.

Seit 2000 zeigt das privat finanzierte International Forum For Visual Dialogues regelmäßig wechselnde Ausstellungen zu bedeutenden zeitgenössischen Fotografen. Das altehrwürdige Kaiserliche Postfuhramt, 2006 ausgebaut von Architekt und Mitbegründer Ingo Pott, bietet den Werken Raum zur Entfaltung und ist zugleich ein Forum für Vorträge und Gespräche mit den Künstlern. Ein Programm, das C/O Berlin weiterverfolgen wird, auch wenn es das Gebäude 2011 verlassen muss.

Depuis 2000, le centre privé organise régulièrement différentes expositions de photographes contemporains de grande renommée. Situé dans le bâtiment de l'ancienne Poste Impériale, réaménagé en 2006 par l'architecte et co-fondateur Ingo Pott, le C/O Berlin présente les œuvres de grands maîtres de la photographie. Le centre organise également des conférences et des forums d'échange avec les artistes. Un programme que le C/O Berlin se promet de poursuivre, même s'il doit quitter le bâtiment en 2011.

Desde el año 2000, el privado International Forum For Visual Dialogues presenta con regularidad diversas exposiciones centradas en destacados fotógrafos contemporáneos. El venerable edificio del correo imperial, renovado en 2006 por el arquitecto y cofundador Ingo Pott, ofrece el espacio ideal para el despliegue de la obra de grandes maestros y es al mismo tiempo un foro en el que escuchar y dialogar con los artistas, un programa que C/O Berlin mantendrá pese a que en 2011 deberá abandonar el edificio.

A

SAMMLUNG BOROS

Reinhardtstraße 20 // Mitte
Tel.: +49 (0)30 27 59 40 65
www.sammlung-boros.de

By appointment
U6 Oranienburger Tor

In 2008, Christian Boros and his wife Karen Lohmann opened a private museum for contemporary art in a World War II–era bunker. The featured artists, including Olafur Eliasson and Tobias Rehberger, installed and staged their works themselves, some of which were created especially for this location. The private collection is open for viewing only on weekends by appointment, which can be made on the Web site.

2008 eröffnete das Ehepaar Christian Boros und Karen Lohmann ein Privatmuseum für zeitgenössische Kunst in einem während des Zweiten Weltkriegs erbauten Hochbunker. Die ausgestellten Künstler, darunter Olafur Eliasson und Tobias Rehberger, haben ihre Exponate, die sie zum Teil eigens für diesen Ort angefertigt haben, in den Räumen selbst installiert und inszeniert. Die Privatsammlung ist nur an Wochenenden nach einer Voranmeldung auf der Website zu besichtigen.

Le couple Christian Boros et Karen Lohmann inaugurèrent en 2008 un musée privé d'art contemporain dans un ancien bunker aérien de la deuxième guerre mondiale. Les œuvres des artistes tel que Olafur Eliasson et Tobias Rehberger y furent en partie créées, installées et mises en scène par leurs soins rien que pour ce musée. Pour visiter la collection privée, il faut s'inscrire à l'avance sur le site.

En 2008, el matrimonio formado por Christian Boros y Karen Lohmann fundó un museo privado de arte contemporáneo en un antiguo búnker de la Segunda Guerra Mundial. Los artistas expuestos, entre ellos Olafur Eliasson y Tobias Rehberger, se ocupan de la instalación y presentación de sus obras, algunas de ellas creadas especialmente para este espacio. Sólo es posible visitar la colección los fines de semana, previa cita concertada a través de la página.

BOROS

Publicist and art patron Christian Boros and his wife Karen Lohmann collect art that originates from and reflects contemporary culture. In this way, they attempt to comprehend their generation's experience of life. The more a work disturbs them, the more keen they are to own it in order to discover the artist's secret. This has made them one of the most influential couples in the German contemporary art scene, with a collection currently comprising around 600 works. Boros started purchasing art at a relatively early age, buying his first piece—a work by Joseph Beuys—with money he received for his high school graduation. While studying under Bazon Brock, Professor of Aesthetics at Wuppertal University, he realized that if he wanted to learn from art, he would also have to "give something back" to it, which is why he began purchasing art while still a student. After establishing a successful advertising agency in Wuppertal, he continued buying more art until he no longer had room in his apartment. This laid the foundation for his collection. He began expanding his repertoire to include installations and sculptures when space had ceased to be an issue. In 2003, he and his wife bought the bunker in order to realize their long-held dream: to live with their art.

Der Werbefachmann und Kunstmäzen Christian Boros sammelt zusammen mit seiner Frau Karen Lohmann Kunst, die dem jeweils aktuellen Zeitgefühl entstammt und dieses widerspiegelt. Auf diese Weise versuchen sie, das Lebensgefühl ihrer Generation zu ergründen. Je mehr sie ein Werk befremdet, desto interessierter waren und sind sie, es zu besitzen, um dem Geheimnis des Künstlers auf die Spur zu kommen. Sie sind so zu einem der einflussreichsten Paare der deutschen zeitgenössischen Kunst geworden, deren Sammlung mittlerweile rund 600 Exponate umfasst. Boros begann früh, Kunst zu kaufen: Mit dem Geld, das er für sein Abitur bekam, erwarb er sein erstes Kunstwerk: eine Arbeit von Joseph Beuys. Während seines Studiums bei Bazon Brock, Professor für Ästhetik an der Universität Wuppertal, lernte er, dass er, wenn er von der Kunst lerne, ihr auch etwas zurückgeben [müsse]". Aus diesem Grund begann er noch während des Studiums mit dem Erwerb von Kunst. Nach der Gründung einer erfolgreichen Werbeagentur in Wuppertal kaufte er immer mehr Kunst, bis die Wohnung sie nicht mehr fassen konnte: Damit war der Grundstein für die Sammlung gelegt. Er erweiterte sein Repertoire um Installationen und Skulpturen, denn die räumlichen Dimensionen waren für ihn nicht mehr von Bedeutung. 2003 kauften er und seine Frau den Hochbunker, um einen lang gehegten Traum zu verwirklichen: mit der Kunst zu leben.

Le publiciste et patron des arts, Christian Boros et sa femme, Karen Lohmann, collectionnent des œuvres d'art contemporain qui reflètent leur époque. C'est leur manière à eux de vivre pleinement leur génération. Pour peu qu'une œuvre leur paraisse des plus insolites, ils doivent et veulent se l'approprier, afin de percer les secrets de l'artiste. C'est ainsi qu'ils sont devenus un des couples les plus influents du monde de l'art contemporain, dont la collection d'œuvres d'art comprend environ 600 pièces d'expositions. La passion de Boros pour l'art commença très tôt, lorsqu'il acheta sa première œuvre avec l'argent reçu lors de son baccalauréat, qui n'était autre qu'une création de Joseph Beuys. Pendant ses études auprès du professeur d'esthétique de l'Université de Wuppertal, Bazon Brock, il apprit à « rendre à l'art ce que l'art nous apporte ». C'est pourquoi il commença dès ses études à acquérir diverses œuvres d'art. Après avoir fondé une agence de publicité prospère à Wuppertal, il multiplia ses acquisitions jusqu'à ce qu'il n'ait plus de place dans son appartement pour les entreposer. Ce fut le point de départ de sa collection privée. Il ne s'arrêta pas en si bon chemin et acheta diverses installations et sculptures, car les notions d'espace n'égalent pas l'importance de l'art à ses yeux. En 2003, ils décidèrent, sa femme et lui, d'acheter un bunker antiaérien afin de réaliser leur plus grand rêve : vivre avec l'art.

El publicista y mecenas de las artes Christian Boros colecciona junto a su esposa Karen Lohmann obras de arte que en su actualidad son reflejo del tiempo en que fueron creadas. De ese modo intentan explorar el concepto vital de su generación. Cuanto más ajena les resulta una pieza, tanto más interesados estaban (y están) en poseerla para a través de ella acceder a los secretos del artista. De este modo se han convertido en una de las parejas más influyentes del arte alemán contemporáneo: su colección abarca ahora cerca de 600 piezas. La afición de Boros comenzó muy pronto: con el dinero recibido tras ganar acceso a la universidad adquirió su primera obra de arte, una pieza de Joseph Beuys. Alumno de Bazon Brock, profesor de estética en la Universidad de Wuppertal, pronto aprendió que al tiempo que aprendía del arte, era preciso también "...devolverle algo". Eso fue lo que le llevó a coleccionar arte incluso durante sus estudios. Tras fundar una exitosa agencia publicitaria en Wuppertal continuó con sus adquisiciones hasta que no fue posible almacenarlas en su vivienda: se pusieron entonces los cimientos de la colección. Amplió su catálogo con instalaciones y esculturas, ya que las dimensiones espaciales habían dejado de ser relevantes para él. En 2003 adquirió junto con su mujer el búnker para hacer realidad un sueño largo tiempo aplazado: convivir con el arte.

CONTEMPORARY FINE ARTS

Am Kupfergraben 10 // Mitte
Tel.: +49 (0)30 2 88 78 70
www.cfa-berlin.com

Tue–Fri 11 am to 6 pm, Sat 11 am to 4 pm
U6, S1, S2, S3, S5, S7, S25, S75 Friedrichstraße

After its establishment in 1992, the gallery of Bruno Brunnet, Nicole Hackert and Philipp Haverkampf occupied a number of locations until 2007, when it finally found a permanent home on the Kupfergraben near the Museum Island. With its light-drenched rooms, David Chipperfield's minimalist building combines a museum-like framework with the charm of a private gallery, making it a worthy space for contemporary works by internationally acclaimed artists such as Daniel Richter and Sarah Lucas.

Gegründet im Jahr 1992, hat die Galerie von Bruno Brunnet, Nicole Hackert und Philipp Haverkampf nach mehreren Standorten im Jahre 2007 ihr neues Domizil am Kupfergraben nahe der Museumsinsel bezogen. David Chipperfields minimalistischer Neubau vereint in seinen lichtdurchfluteten Räumen einen musealen Rahmen mit dem Charme einer privaten Galerie und garantiert so eine angemessene Präsentation der zeitgenössischen Werke bekannter Künstler wie Daniel Richter oder Sarah Lucas.

Après plusieurs déménagements, la galerie de Bruno Brunnet, Nicole Hackert et Philipp Haverkampf, fondée en 1992, a finalement élu domicile en 2007 au Kupfergraben, dans les alentours de l'île aux musées. L'architecte David Chipperfield a su combiner, au sein de ce bâtiment minimaliste aux espaces lumineux, le cadre d'un musée aux charmes d'une galerie privée afin de présenter au mieux les œuvres contemporaines d'artistes de renommée internationale tels que Daniel Richter ou Sarah Lucas.

Fundada en 1992, y tras ocupar otros espacios, la galería de Bruno Brunnet, Nicole Hackert y Philipp Haverkampf se instaló finalmente en 2007 en el local de Kupfergraben, cerca de la Isla de los Museos. El moderno y minimalista edificio de David Chipperfield aúna en sus luminosas salas el marco museístico ideal con el encanto de una galería privada, y garantiza de ese modo la idónea presentación de las obras contemporáneas de artistas internacionales tan conocidos como Daniel Richter o Sarah Lucas.

Opened in 2006 and situated at Pariser Platz, the museum houses one of the world's largest collections on the history of the famous American political family. Photographs from the collection of Camera Work AG, along with films, official documents and personal items give visitors an intimate glimpse of the Kennedys' life and influence. Special thematic exhibits and events round out the experience.

Am Pariser Platz gelegen, beherbergt das 2006 eröffnete Museum eine der weltweit größten Sammlungen zur Geschichte der bekannten amerikanischen Politikerfamilie. Fotografien aus der Sammlung der Camera Work AG, ergänzt durch Filme, offizielle Dokumente und persönliche Gegenstände, geben dem Besucher einen intimen Einblick in das Leben und Wirken der Kennedys. Themenverwandte Sonderausstellungen und Events erweitern das Angebot.

Situé sur la Pariser Platz, ce musée, inauguré en 2006, abrite une des plus grandes collections au monde de pièces relatant l'histoire de cette célèbre famille américaine. Le visiteur sera transporté dans le monde des Kennedy à travers des clichés de la Camera Work AG, complétée par des projections, des documents officiels et des objets personnels afin de mieux comprendre son histoire et son influence. Des expositions temporaires et divers événements complètent cette rétrospective biographique.

En el Pariser Platz se encuentra este museo fundado en 2006, y alberga la mayor colección mundial centrada en la conocida familia de políticos estadounidenses. Las fotografías de la colección de Camera Work AG, complementadas con filmaciones, documentos oficiales y objetos personales, permiten al visitante acercarse a la vida y la obra de los Kennedy. La oferta se completa con exposiciones y eventos temáticos.

MUSEUM THE KENNEDYS

Pariser Platz 4 // Mitte
Tel.: +49 (0)30 20 65 35 70
www.thekennedys.de

Daily 10 am to 6 pm
U55, S1, S2, S25 Brandenburger Tor

A

Since 2006, Thomas Schulte has shown contemporary art at Tuteur Haus, redesigned in 1912–13 by Hermann Muthesius. Established in 1991 in the Charlottenburg district as Galerie Franck + Schulte, the gallery emphasizes the presentation of conceptual art from 1960 to the present. Paintings, photographs, graphic arts, as well as sculptures and installations by such artists as Richard Deacon, Robert Mapplethorpe, Peter Rogiers, Katharina Sieverding, and Robert Wilson are shown in changing exhibitions.

Seit 2006 zeigt Thomas Schulte im von Hermann Muthesius 1912/13 umgestalteten Tuteur Haus zeitgenössische Kunst. Der Schwerpunkt der 1991 in Berlin Charlottenburg als Galerie Franck + Schulte gegründeten Galerie liegt auf der Präsentation konzeptioneller Kunst von 1960 bis heute. Malerei, Fotografien, Grafiken sowie Plastiken und Installationen von Künstlern wie Richard Deacon, Robert Mapplethorpe, Peter Rogiers, Katharina Sieverding, Robert Wilson werden in wechselnden Ausstellungen gezeigt.

La galerie d'art contemporain de Thomas Schulte est située depuis 2006 dans la Tuteur Haus, qui fut transformée en 1912/13 par l'architecte Hermann Muthesius. Cette galerie, fondée en 1991 à Charlottenburg et originellement connue comme la Galerie Franck + Schulte, est spécialisée dans l'art conceptuel de 1960 à nos jours. Des peintures, des photographies, des graphiques, des arts plastiques et des installations d'artistes comme Richard Deacon, Robert Mapplethorpe, Peter Rogiers, Katharina Sieverding, Robert Wilson y sont exposés.

Thomas Schulte expone arte contemporáneo desde 2006 en Tuteur Haus, la villa rediseñada por Hermann Muthesius en 1912/13. El principal interés de la galería, inaugurada en 1991 como Galerie Franck + Schulte en Charlottenburg, se centra en la presentación de arte conceptual desde 1960 hasta la actualidad. Sus salas han acogido pinturas, fotografías, obra gráfica, esculturas e instalaciones de artistas como Richard Deacon, Robert Mapplethorpe, Peter Rogiers, Katharina Sieverding y Robert Wilson.

GALERIE THOMAS SCHULTE

Charlottenstraße 24 // Mitte
Tel.: +49 (0)30 20 60 89 90
www.galeriethomasschulte.de

Tue–Sat noon to 6 pm and by appointment
U2, U6 Stadtmitte

GALERIE ULRICH FIEDLER

Charlottenstraße 68–71 // Mitte
Tel.: +49 (0)30 33 09 40 10
www.ulrichfiedler.com

By appointment
U2, U6 Stadtmitte

After 22 years in Cologne, Ulrich Fiedler moved his gallery to Berlin's Mitte district. Specializing in classic modern furniture, the assortment is directed at passionate collectors with a weakness for special antiques, but primarily international museums. Based on years of experience, Fiedler puts together pieces that tell the history of design—but also come at a price. Together with Thomas Taubert, he also runs the ftc. gallery for contemporary art in Kreuzberg.

Nach 22 Jahren in Köln ist Ulrich Fiedler mit seiner Galerie nach Berlin Mitte gezogen. Spezialisiert auf Möbel der Klassischen Moderne, richtet sich das Sortiment an leidenschaftliche Sammler mit einem Faible für besondere Antiquitäten, vor allem aber internationale Museen. Basierend auf jahrelangen Erfahrungen, stellt Fiedler Exponate zusammen, die Designgeschichte erzählen, allerdings auch ihren Preis haben. Zusammen mit Thomas Taubert betreibt er zudem die Galerie für zeitgenössische Kunst ftc. in Kreuzberg.

Après 22 ans passés à Cologne, Ulrich Fiedler a délocalisé sa galerie dans le centre de Berlin. Spécialisée dans les meubles de la Classique Moderne, la collection s'adresse à des collectionneurs passionnés, ayant un faible pour les antiquités spéciales et les musées internationaux. Grâce à ses longues années d'expérience, Fiedler a rassemblé des pièces d'expositions qui racontent l'histoire du design, mais qui ont également leur prix. En collaboration avec Thomas Taubert, il tient également la galerie d'art contemporain ftc. à Kreuzberg.

Tras 22 años en Colonia, Ulrich Fiedler ha trasladado su galería a Berlin Mitte. Especializado en muebles modernos aunque clásicos, su catálogo se dirige especialmente a coleccionistas con cierta debilidad por las antigüedades fuera de lo común, así como a museos internacionales. A partir de su amplísima experiencia, Fiedler presenta sus piezas en combinaciones que narran la historia del diseño, y que por supuesto tienen su precio. Junto con Thomas Taubert dirige también la galería de arte contemporáneo ftc. en Kreuzberg.

ART 33

2000
1990

2009 PETER LORENZ
LEVERKUSEN
BERLIN
ROZWAR

EAST SIDE GALLERY

Mühlenstraße 70–71 // Friedrichshain
Tel.: +49 (0)30 2 51 71 59
www.eastsidegallery.com

U1 Warschauer Straße,
S3, S5, S7, S75 Warschauer Straße, Ostbahnhof

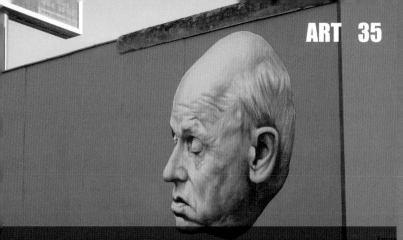

One of the most famous and largest relics from the time of Berlin's division into East and West is the longest remaining section of the Berlin Wall. This 4,318-ft.-long segment extending from the Ostbahnhof to the Oberbaumbrücke forms the world's longest open-air gallery. Since its restoration in 2009, a majority of the artwork dating from 1990 when the gallery was first established have been repainted by the original artists at their same locations.

Eines der bekanntesten und größten Relikte aus der Zeit der Teilung Berlins in Ost und West ist das längste erhaltene Stück der Berliner Mauer. Es erstreckt sich zwischen Ostbahnhof und Oberbaumbrücke auf 1 316 m und bildet die längste Open-Air-Galerie der Welt. Nach der Sanierung im Jahre 2009 wurde der Großteil der Kunstwerke aus dem Gründungsjahr der Galerie, 1990, von den ursprünglichen Künstlern an gleicher Stelle wieder angebracht.

L'East Side Gallery, un des vestiges les plus connus du temps où Berlin était encore divisée en deux secteurs, est la plus longue section du Mur encore sur pied qui sert de support à une exposition d'œuvres d'art. D'une longueur de 1 316 m, il s'étend de la Ostbahnhof au Oberbaumbrücke et représente la plus longue galerie en plein air du monde. Après son assainissement en 2009, la majorité des œuvres datant de la fondation de la galerie, en 1990, furent rétablies à la même place par leurs artistes originaux.

Una de las reliquias más conocidas y voluminosas que han sobrevivido a la época en la que Berlín estaba dividida en sectores es el mayor tramo conservado del Muro de Berlín. Se extiende a lo largo de 1 316 m, desde Ostbahnhof hasta Oberbaumbrücke, y se ha convertido en la galería al aire libre más larga del mundo. Tras las obras de rehabilitación de 2009 los artistas originales procedieron a la reproducción en el mismo espacio de la mayoría de obras creadas en 1990, año de fundación de la galería.

A

BERLINISCHE GALERIE

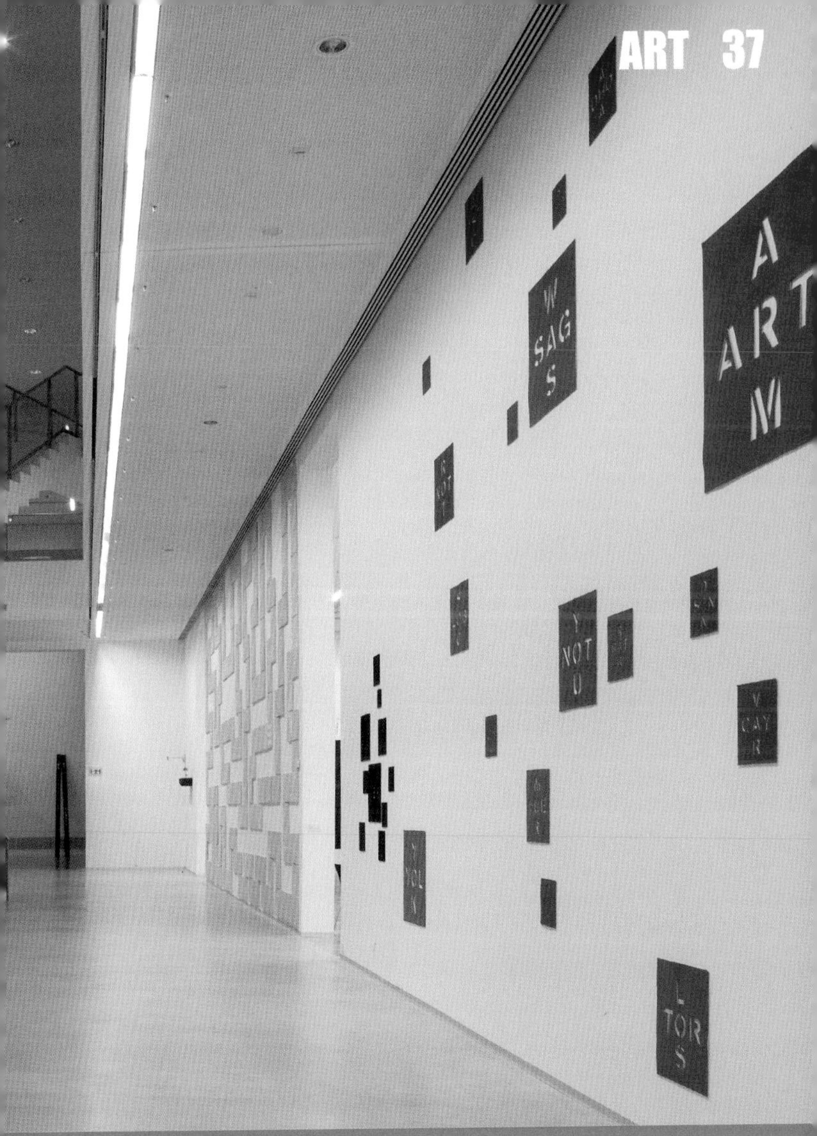
A
ART
M
W
SAG
S
Y
NOT
U
TOR
S

Founded in 1975 as a private association and becoming a foundation in 1994, this gallery's mission has been to collect and exhibit Berlin's own fine art, photography and architecture dating from 1870 to the present. Its permanent and special exhibitions feature, for example, works by Berlin's secessionists and expressionists, Junge Wilde, neo-objectivists, and contemporary artists. Since 2004, the collection has been housed in a former warehouse that was converted into a museum.

1975 als Verein gegründet und 1994 in eine Stiftung umgewandelt, widmet sich diese der Sammlung und Präsentation von Werken aus bildender Kunst, Fotografie und Architektur in Berlin von 1870 bis heute. In Dauer- und Sonderausstellungen werden unter anderem Arbeiten der Berliner Sezession, des Expressionismus, der Jungen Wilden, der Neuen Sachlichkeit und der zeitgenössischen Kunst gezeigt. Seit 2004 wird die Sammlung in einer als Museum umgestalteten ehemaligen Lagerhalle präsentiert.

Créée en 1975, la Berlinische Galerie, initialement une association, est devenue une fondation en 1994 dont les œuvres exposées sont dédiées aux beaux-arts, à la photographie et à l'architecture berlinoise de 1870 à nos jours. La collection permanente et les expositions temporaires présentent les œuvres de l'association Berliner Sezession, de l'expressionisme, du mouvement Junge Wilde, de la Nouvelle Objectivité et de l'art contemporain. La collection permanente est exposée depuis 2004 dans un ancien hangar réaménagé en musée.

Fundada como asociación en 1975 y transformada en fundación en 1994, la galería se concentra en la colección y presentación de obras de las artes plásticas, la fotografía y la arquitectura berlinesas desde 1870 hasta la actualidad. Sus exposiciones permanentes y especiales han estado dedicadas, entre otros, a la Secesión berlinesa, el expresionismo, los Junge Wilde, la Nueva Objetividad y el arte contemporáneo. Desde 2004, la colección está expuesta en un antiguo almacén reconvertido en museo.

BERLINISCHE GALERIE

Alte Jakobstraße 128 // Kreuzberg
Tel.: +49 (0)30 78 90 26 00
www.berlinischegalerie.de

Wed–Mon 10 am to 6 pm
U6 Kochstraße

MARTIN-GROPIUS-BAU

Niederkirchnerstraße 7 // Kreuzberg
Tel.: +49 (0)30 25 48 60
www.gropiusbau.de

Daily 10 am to 8 pm
U2, S1, S2, S25 Potsdamer Platz

1978 saw the beginning of the reconstruction of this landmarked, Neorenaissance-style building with its central atrium. A former museum of applied arts that suffered extensive damage during World War II, today the Martin-Gropius-Bau hosts 15 to 20 temporary exhibits annually from a variety of fields including art, photography, archeology, and artist retrospectives. A bookstore, conference room, cinema hall, and the Gropius restaurant complete the overall picture.

Nachdem das im Stil der Renaissance erbaute einstige Kunstgewerbemuseum mit seinem zentralen Lichthof im Zweiten Weltkrieg schwer beschädigt wurde, begann 1978 die Wiederherstellung des denkmalgeschützten Bauwerks. Heute wird in dem Haus in 15 bis 20 wechselnden Ausstellungen jährlich ein breites Spektrum aus Kunst, Fotografie, Archäologie und Künstlerretrospektiven geboten. Eine Buchhandlung, ein Vortrags- und Kinosaal sowie das Restaurant Gropius ergänzt das Angebot.

Classé monument historique, ce musée des arts décoratifs de style néorenaissance avec sa cour intérieure centrale, considérablement endommagé lors de la seconde guerre mondiale, fut rénové et réaménagé en 1978. De nos jours, le Martin-Gropius-Bau à Berlin organise annuellement 15 à 20 expositions variées sur l'art, la photographie, l'archéologie et des rétrospectives d'artistes. Il abrite également une librairie, une salle de conférences et de cinéma ainsi que le restaurant Gropius.

La Segunda Guerra Mundial ocasionó enormes destrozos en el antiguo Museo de las Artes Aplicadas, de estilo neorenacentista y dotado de un patio de luces central. En 1978 comenzaron las obras de restauración de este edificio, declarado monumento nacional. Actualmente, en él se organizan entre 15 y 20 exposiciones cada año, que abarcan un amplísimo espectro de arte, fotografía, arqueología y retrospectivas de artistas. Cuenta además con una librería, un salón de actos y el restaurante Gropius.

The museum building, inspired in form by an ancient podium temple and completed in 1968 using plans by Ludwig Mies van der Rohe, is part of Berlin's State Museum system and the Kulturforum at Potsdamer Platz. Boasting the world's largest self-supporting steel sheet as a roof, the all-glass main hall is at once an architectural attraction and location for temporary exhibitions. The lower level houses the permanent exhibit with works of European painting and sculpture from classic modernism to the 1960s.

Das an einen antiken Podiumtempel angelehnte, 1968 nach Plänen von Ludwig Mies van der Rohe fertiggestellte Museumsgebäude ist Teil der Staatlichen Museen zu Berlin und des Kulturforums am Potsdamer Platz. Mit der weltweit größten freitragenden Stahlplatte als Dach ist die vollständig verglaste Haupthalle zugleich architektonischer Anziehungspunkt und Ort für temporäre Ausstellungen. Im Untergeschoss ist die Dauerausstellung mit Werken der europäischen Malerei und Plastik von der Klassischen Moderne bis zu den 1960er Jahren untergebracht.

Ce bâtiment formel, rappelant un temple antique dressé sur un podium, fut conçu en 1968 d'après les plans de Ludwig Mies van der Rohe et fait partie des musées nationaux de Berlin et du Kulturforum de la Potsdamer Platz. Ce joyau architectonique, composé d'un toit indépendant en acier et d'un hall principal entièrement vitré, attire beaucoup de visiteurs et abrite diverses expositions temporaires. L'exposition permanente située au sous-sol présente des œuvres de la peinture et des arts plastiques européennes de la période Classique Moderne à 1960.

El edificio del museo, construido en 1968 a partir de los planes de Ludwig Mies van der Rohe y cuya forma se inspira en los antiguos templos, forma parte de los museos estatales de Berlín y del Kulturforum de Potsdamer Platz. La sala principal, que tiene por techo la mayor plancha de acero autoportante del mundo, es a un tiempo pieza de interés arquitectónico y espacio de exposiciones temporales. En el sótano se aloja la exposición permanente, con obras de la pintura y escultura europeas desde el modernismo hasta la década de 1960.

NEUE NATIONALGALERIE

Potsdamer Straße 50 // Tiergarten
Tel.: +49 (0)30 2 66 42 30 40
www.neue-nationalgalerie.de

Tue+Wed+Fri 10 am to 6 pm, Thu 10 am to 10 pm,
Sat+Sun 11 am to 6 pm
U2, S1, S2, S25 Potsdamer Platz

HAMBURGER BAHNHOF
MUSEUM FÜR GEGENWART BERLIN

Invalidenstraße 50–51 // Tiergarten
Tel.: +49 (0)30 3 97 83 40
www.hamburgerbahnhof.de

Tue–Fri 10 am to 6 pm, Sat 11 am to 8 pm, Sun 11 am to 6 pm
U5, S3, S5, S7, S75 Hauptbahnhof

Since 1996, a former terminal station has been home to the Museum for Contemporary Art. Based on private collections from Erich Marx, Friedrich Christian Flick and Egidio Marzona with additional pieces from the Nationalgalerie, this internationally acclaimed museum offers an overview of contemporary art in an exhibition space measuring 3.2 acres. Its many highlights include the blue and green light installation by American artist Dan Flavin that illuminates the Neoclassical façade.

Im Gebäude des ehemaligen Kopfbahnhofs befindet sich seit 1996 das Museum für Gegenwart. Basierend auf Privatsammlungen von Erich Marx, Friedrich Christian Flick und Egidio Marzona, die durch die Sammlung der Nationalgalerie ergänzt werden, gibt das international renommierte Museum auf 13 000 m² einen Überblick über die zeitgenössische Kunst. Die blau-grüne Lichtinstallation des amerikanischen Künstlers Dan Flavin an der neoklassizistischen Fassade zählt zu den Attraktionen des Museums.

L'ancienne gare terminus de ligne abrite depuis 1996 le musée d'art contemporain Hamburger Bahnhof. Ce musée de renommée internationale d'une superficie de 13 000 m², où sont exposées les collections privées d'Erich Marx, Friedrich Christian Flick et Egidio Marzona, complétées par celle de la galerie nationale, donne un aperçu de l'art contemporain. L'installation dichromatique (bleu-vert) conçue par l'artiste américain Dan Flavin, ajoutée à la façade néoclassique, compte parmi les attractions du musée.

En 1996 se instaló en el edificio de la antigua estación terminal un museo de arte contemporáneo. Sobre la base de las colecciones privadas de Erich Marx, Friedrich Christian Flick y Egidio Marzona, complementadas con las piezas de la galería nacional, se articula un extenso recorrido por el arte contemporáneo a lo largo de los 13 000 m² de este museo de renombre mundial. La instalación lumínica en verde y azul del artista estadounidense Dan Flavin sobre la fachada neoclasicista es un atractivo más del museo.

A

HELMUT NEWTON STIFTUNG
IM MUSEUM FÜR FOTOGRAFIE

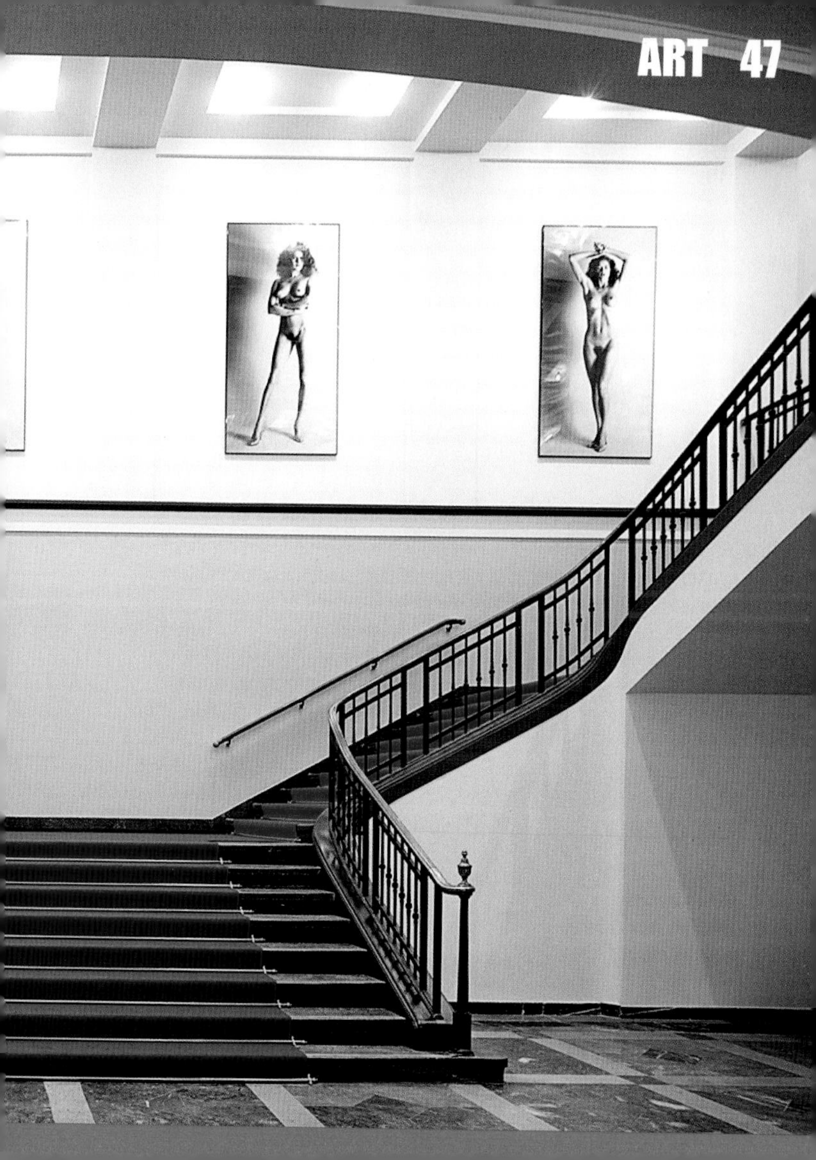

A

More than just a monument to the achievements of Helmut and June Newton, the museum hosts regular exhibitions by other photo artists whose works enter into a dialog with the sometimes provocative works of Helmut Newton. In addition, this building located behind the Zoo train station is itself steeped in history: it was originally a casino for Prussian officers. The photographic collection from the National Museum's Art Library is exhibited in the restored Emperor's Hall on the third floor.

Mehr als nur ein Museum über die Lebenswerke von Helmut und June Newton, finden hier regelmäßig Ausstellungen zu anderen Fotokünstlern statt, deren Arbeiten in einen Dialog mit den bisweilen provokativen Werken Helmut Newtons gebracht werden. Nicht nur die Sammlung selbst, sondern auch das Gebäude hinter dem Bahnhof Zoo ist geschichtsträchtig. Früher befand sich darin ein preußisches Offizierskasino. Im restaurierten Kaisersaal im zweiten Stock präsentiert sich die Sammlung Fotografie der Kunstbibliothek.

Cette fondation est bien plus qu'un musée présentant les œuvres d'Helmut et June Newton. On peut également, lors d'expositions régulières, y admirer les œuvres d'autres photographes ayant un rapport avec les œuvres provocantes d'Helmut Newton. Tout comme sa collection, le bâtiment situé derrière le Bahnhof Zoo est également chargé d'histoire : on y trouvait à l'époque un casino destiné aux officiers prussiens. Dans la Salle Impériale restaurée du 2e étage se trouve la collection de photographies de la Bibliothèque des Beaux-Arts.

Mucho más que un museo sobre la obra de Helmut y June Newton: aquí se organizan con regularidad exposiciones de otros artistas fotográficos, cuyas piezas se instalan en animado diálogo con las en ocasiones provocadoras imágenes de Helmut Newton. No sólo la colección, sino también el edificio a espaldas de Bahnhof Zoo está cargado de historia: en otra época fue sede de un club de oficiales prusianos. En la restaurada Sala Imperial de la segunda planta está alojada la colección fotográfica de la Biblioteca de las Artes.

HELMUT NEWTON STIFTUNG
IM MUSEUM FÜR FOTOGRAFIE

Jebensstraße 2 // Charlottenburg
Tel.: +49 (0)30 31 86 48 56
www.helmutnewton.com

Tue–Sun 10 am to 6 pm, Thu 10 am to 10 pm
U2, U9, S3, S5, S7, S75 Zoologischer Garten

On an idyllic rear courtyard in Charlottenburg, this gallery named after Alfred Stieglitz's magazine houses the world's most comprehensive archived collection of photographs and photography books on two floors. With temporary exhibitions of the works of such iconic figures as Irving Penn, Diane Arbus and Richard Avedon, of well-known representatives from the contemporary scene, and of up-and-coming artists, visitors are treated to a comprehensive cross-section of the world of photography.

In einem idyllischen Hinterhof in Charlottenburg beherbergt die nach Alfred Stieglitz' gleichnamiger Zeitschrift benannte Galerie auf zwei Etagen eine der weltweit umfangreichsten archivierten Sammlungen von Fotografien und Fotobildbänden. Werke von Ikonen wie Irving Penn, Diane Arbus und Richard Avedon, von namhaften Vertretern der aktuellen Szene sowie Arbeiten neuer Talente vermitteln dem Besucher in wechselnden Ausstellungen eine umfassende Übersicht über die Welt der Fotografie.

La galerie, nommée d'après le magazine d'Alfred Stieglitz, est située dans une arrière-cour du Charlottenburg et abrite sur deux étages une des plus grandes sections d'archives de photographies et de volumes illustrés au monde. Le visiteur se retrouve propulsé dans le monde de la photographie à travers différentes expositions, faisant honneur à des icônes comme Irving Penn, Diane Arbus et Richard Avedon, à des artistes contemporains ainsi qu'aux nouveaux talents.

Un idílico patio trasero de Charlottenburg acoge la galería bautizada con el nombre de la revista fundada por Alfred Stieglitz. Distribuida en dos pisos, alberga libros de fotografía y una de las colecciones fotográficas más extensas de todo el mundo. Las variadas exposiciones de iconos como Irving Penn, Diane Arbus y Richard Avedon, de destacados representantes modernos de la profesión y de jóvenes talentos permiten al visitante adentrarse en el mundo de la fotografía.

E HUYN

CAMERA WORK

Kantstraße 149 // Charlottenburg
Tel.: +49 (0)30 3 10 07 73
www.camerawork.de

Tue–Sat 11 am to 6 pm
U1 Uhlandstraße, S3, S5, S7, S75 Savignyplatz

A

HAUS AM WALDSEE

HAUS AM WALDSEE

Argentinische Allee 30 // Zehlendorf
Tel.: +49 (0)30 8 01 89 35
www.hausamwaldsee.de

Tue–Sun 11 am to 6 pm, Wed 11 am to 8 pm
U3 Krumme Lanke

After 1945 this villa became one of the first cultural venues for presentations of contemporary art, theater and music in a devastated Berlin. It's where the Berlin Philharmonic gave its first postwar concert and has since become a space for exhibitions by internationally known modern artists such as Käthe Kollwitz, Niki de Saint Phalle and Norbert Bisky, regularly accompanied by concerts and workshops. The garden provides space for larger exhibits, such as Werner Aisslinger's Loftcube.

Nach 1945 zählte die Villa zu den ersten Kultureinrichtungen, die zeitgenössische Kunst, Theater und Musik im zerstörten Berlin präsentierten. So gaben die Berliner Philharmoniker hier ihr erstes Nachkriegskonzert. Seither hat sich das Haus zu einem Ort für Ausstellungen international renommierter Künstler der Moderne wie Niki de Saint Phalle und Norbert Bisky entwickelt, die regelmäßig von Konzerten und Workshops begleitete werden. Der Garten bietet Platz für große Exponate wie Werner Aisslingers Loftcube.

La villa compte depuis 1945 parmi les premiers lieux culturels présentant des œuvres d'art contemporain, de théâtre et de musique du Berlin en ruine. C'est ici que l'Orchestre philarmonique de Berlin donna son premier concert d'après-guerre. La villa est devenue depuis lors un lieu d'expositions, de concerts et d'ateliers où sont présentées les œuvres d'artistes tels que Niki de Saint Phalle et Norbert Bisky. Le jardin de la villa est un lieu parfait pour admirer des créations telles que le Loftcube de Werner Aisslinger.

Tras 1945, la villa fue de las primeras en presentar arte, música y teatro contemporáneos en el Berlín destruido por la guerra. La Filarmónica de Berlín ofreció allí su primer concierto de posguerra. Desde entonces el edificio ha devenido un espacio de exposición para artistas de renombre internacional como Niki de Saint Phalle y Norbert Bisky, al tiempo que mantiene un programa regular de conciertos y talleres. Los jardines ofrecen el espacio necesario para piezas como el Loftcube de Werner Aisslinger.

ARCHIT

The architecture of Berlin reflects the city's turbulent history. Baroque and Neoclassical edifices by the great Prussian master builders, the houses from the Gründerzeit period, and modern architecture—all these style epochs influence the face of the city. But structures from the Nazi era and the postwar period are also everywhere. It was not until the fall of the Berlin Wall that a phase of reconstruction became possible in the heart of the city unlike any metropolis had experienced before. Large-scale projects like Potsdamer Platz, the government district and the main railway station have dominated the last two decades. Revitalization of such tradition-laden locations as Pariser Platz at the Brandenburg Gate engendered debates about dealing with buildings from the past. Constructive discussions resulted in exemplary solutions where consistent modern architecture and the preservation of historical structures were no longer considered opposites. An eloquent testimony of this is David Chipperfield's renovation of the war-ravaged Neue Museum.

Die Architektur Berlins spiegelt die turbulente Geschichte der Stadt wider. Barocke und klassizistische Bauten der großen preußischen Baumeister, die Häuser der Gründerzeit und die Architektur des Neuen Bauens – all diese verschiedenen Stilepochen prägen das Stadtbild. Aber auch die Bauwerke des Nationalsozialismus und der Nachkriegszeit sind allgegenwärtig. Doch erst der Mauerfall machte einen Umbau im Herzen der Stadt möglich, wie ihn zuvor kaum eine Millionenstadt erlebt hat. Großprojekte wie der Potsdamer Platz, das Regierungsviertel oder der Hauptbahnhof bestimmten die vergangenen zwei Jahrzehnte. Revitalisierungen traditionsreicher Orte wie des Pariser Platzes vor dem Brandenburger Tor wurden von kontroversen Diskussionen um den Umgang mit der baulichen Vergangenheit begleitet. Fruchtbare Debatten, die zu beispielhaften Lösungen geführt haben, bei denen konsequente moderne Architektur und die Bewahrung historischer Bausubstanz keine Gegensätze mehr bilden müssen, wovon David Chipperfields Renovierung des kriegszerstörten Neuen Museums beredtes Zeugnis ablegt.

L'architecture de Berlin reflète l'histoire mouvementée de la ville. Edifices de style baroque et classique des grands maîtres prussiens, maisons et villas du « Gründerzeit » et architecture moderne de la Nouvelle Objectivité : différentes périodes caractérisées par des styles architecturaux s'inscrivent dans le paysage urbain. Même les ouvrages de l'époque du national-socialisme et de l'après-guerre parsèment la ville. Ce n'est cependant qu'à la chute du mur que le cœur de la ville connut de profondes transformations comme aucune autre grande métropole. Des projets de grande envergure comme la Potsdamer Platz, le quartier du gouvernement ou encore la gare centrale ont marqué les deux dernières décennies. Des travaux de réhabilitation de sites chargés d'histoire tels que la Pariser Platz située juste devant la porte de Brandebourg ont fait l'objet de vives controverses portant sur une conciliation avec le passé architectural. Des débats fructueux ont débouché sur des solutions exemplaires visant à établir une harmonie entre une architecture moderne rigoureuse et la conservation du patrimoine bâti. Un défi relevé avec brio par David Chipperfield qui s'est vu confier la rénovation du Neues Museum endommagé pendant la Seconde Guerre mondiale.

La arquitectura de Berlín refleja la turbulenta historia de la ciudad. Los edificios barrocos y clasicistas de los grandes constructores prusianos, las casas del siglo XIX, la arquitectura de la Nueva Construcción. Muchos son los estilos que definen la imagen de la ciudad. Pero también las construcciones del nacional-socialismo y la posguerra son omnipresentes; sin embargo, sólo la caída del Muro hizo posible la remodelación del corazón de la ciudad, que ha experimentado un cambio sin parangón entre las grandes capitales. Los extensísimos proyectos de Potsdamer Platz, la zona del gobierno y la estación central han sido la constante en la ciudad durante los dos últimos decenios. La revitalización de espacios tan tradicionales como Pariser Platz en la Puerta de Brandenburgo ha ido acompañada de controversias relativas al respeto por el pasado arquitectónico, un debate fructífero que ha dado lugar a ejemplares soluciones en las que la arquitectura moderna y la conservación del aura histórica no deben necesariamente constituir conceptos enfrentados como demuestra a la perfección la renovación acometida por David Chipperfield del Neues Museum, destruido durante la guerra.

A

Aedes is considered a leading international institution for communicating architectural culture. Drawing on 30 years' experience, Kristin Feireiss and her team promote young talent by means of exhibitions and catalogs. Renowned architects such as Rem Koolhaas, Daniel Libeskind and Zaha Hadid were exhibited here before they achieved world fame. In addition to its facilities in Prenzlauer Berg, Aedes also has a gallery devoted to landscape architecture in Charlottenburg.

Aedes gilt als eine der international führenden Institutionen, wenn es um die Vermittlung von Baukultur geht. Kristin Feireiss und ihr Team fördern, gestützt auf ihre 30-jährigen Erfahrungen, junge Talente der Szene mit Ausstellungen und Katalogen. Namhafte Architekten wie Rem Koolhaas, Daniel Libeskind und Zaha Hadid präsentierten ihre Arbeiten bereits, bevor sie weltbekannt wurden. Zusätzlich zu den Räumen in Prenzlauer Berg unterhält Aedes in Charlottenburg noch eine Galerie für Landschaftsarchitektur.

L'Aedes compte parmi les hauts-lieux de la culture architecturale. Kristin Feireiss y met à profit ses 30 ans d'expérience pour promouvoir de jeunes talents, en y organisant des expositions et en présentant une série de catalogues. Des artistes notables tels que Rem Koolhaas, Daniel Libeskind et Zaha Hadid y exposaient déjà leurs œuvres avant de devenir mondialement connus. Hormis les salles d'expositions du quartier Prenzlauer Berg, l'Aedes entretient également une galerie d'architecture paysagère dans le quartier de Charlottenburg.

Aedes pasa por ser una de las instituciones de referencia internacional en cuanto a cultura arquitectónica. Desde la autoridad de sus 30 años de experiencia, Kristin Feireiss y su equipo promocionan con exposiciones y catálogos a jóvenes talentos. Destacados arquitectos como Rem Koolhaas, Daniel Libeskind y Zaha Hadid presentaron aquí sus obras antes de ser conocidos mundialmente. Además de las dependencias en Prenzlauer Berg, Aedes dirige en Charlottenburg otra galería centrada en arquitectura paisajística.

AEDES AM PFEFFERBERG

Christinenstraße 18 // Mitte
Tel.: +49 (0)30 2 82 70 15
www.aedes-arc.de

Tue–Fri 11 am to 6.30 pm, Sat+Sun 11 am to 7 pm
U2 Senefelderplatz

A

NEUES MUSEUM

NEUES MUSEUM

Bodestraße 1 // Mitte
Tel.: +49 (0)30 2 66 42 42 42
www.neues-museum.de

Mon–Wed, Sun 10 am to 6 pm, Thu–Sat 10 am to 8 pm
U6, S1, S2, S3, S5, S7, S25, S75 Friedrichstraße,
S3, S5, S7, S75 Hackescher Markt

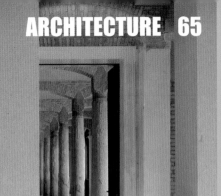

Almost 65 years after suffering serious damage in World War II, the Neues Museum reopened in 2009. David Chipperfield restored the 19th-century Stüler building, reconstructing parts of the original interior architecture and adding modern elements such as the central staircase. The over 5-acre building brings together the Museum for Prehistory and Early History, pieces from the Antiquities Collection, and the Egyptian Museum—including its most famous exhibit, the bust of Nefertiti.

Fast 65 Jahre nach seiner starken Zerstörung im Zweiten Weltkrieg wurde das Neue Museum 2009 wiedereröffnet. David Chipperfield hat den Stüler-Bau aus dem 19. Jahrhundert restauriert, Teile der originalen Innenarchitektur wiederhergestellt und durch moderne Elemente, wie die zentrale Treppenanlage, gelungen ergänzt. Das mehr als 20 500 m² große Haus vereint das Museum für Vor- und Frühgeschichte, Teile der Antikensammlung und das Ägyptische Museum, dessen berühmtestes Exponat die Büste der Nofretete ist.

En ruine pendant 65 ans après sa destruction pendant la Seconde Guerre mondiale, le Neues Museum a rouvert ses portes en 2009. David Chipperfield a restauré ce bâtiment du XIXe siècle de l'architecte Stüler, en y modernisant une partie de l'architecture intérieure d'origine, comme le rappelle l'escalier central. Ce musée abrite sur une surface de 20 500 m² le musée de la Préhistoire et de la Protohistoire, certaines œuvres de l'Antiquité ainsi que le musée égyptien, dont la pièce maîtresse est le buste de Néfertiti.

En 2009, casi 65 años después de los graves desperfectos sufridos durante la Segunda Guerra Mundial el museo abría de nuevo sus puertas. David Chipperfield ha restaurado el decimonónico edificio de Stüler, recuperando en parte el interiorismo original y complementándolo a la perfección con elementos modernos como la escalinata central. Sobre los más de 20 500 m² del edificio conviven el museo de la prehistoria y la historia antigua, partes de la colección de antigüedades y el museo egipcio, con el famoso busto de Nefertiti.

JACOB-UND-WILHELM-GRIMM-ZENTRUM

Geschwister-Scholl-Straße 3 // Mitte
Tel.: +49 (0)30 2 09 39 93 70
www.grimm-zentrum.hu-berlin.de

Mon–Fri 8 am to midnight, Sat+Sun 10 am to 6 pm
U6, S1, S2, S3, S5, S7, S25, S75 Friedrichstraße

Completed in 2009, the new building of the main library of Humboldt-Universität is generously proportioned in every aspect. In his geometric design inspired by classic modern architecture, Max Dudler combines workspaces and media rooms, a café, an auditorium, and the main computer and media center, in addition to the library with its roughly 2.5 million volumes. The heart of the building is the terraced reading room extending across all five levels of the open stacks that is lit by an enormous glass roof.

In jeder Hinsicht großzügig angelegt ist der 2009 fertiggestellte Neubau der Zentralbibliothek der Humboldt-Universität. Max Dudler vereint in seinem von der Architektur der Moderne inspirierten, geometrischen Entwurf neben der Bibliothek mit ca. 2,5 Millionen Bänden auch Arbeits- und Medienräume, eine Cafeteria, ein Auditorium und das zentrale Computer- und Medienzentrum. Das Herzstück des Hauses ist der terrassenartig angelegte Lesesaal, der sich über alle fünf Stockwerke des Freihandbereichs erstreckt und von einem enormen Glasdach erhellt wird.

La bibliothèque de l'université Humboldt, achevée en 2009, présente à tous égards une architecture généreuse. Max Dudler a conçu ce joyau architectural en s'inspirant du style de la Classique Moderne. L'édifice abrite, en plus de la bibliothèque et ses 2,5 millions d'ouvrages, des aires de travail, des salles de média, une cafétéria, un auditoire et le centre principal d'informatique et des médias. La salle de lecture en forme de terrasse avec son énorme toit vitré, surplombant les cinq étages de la bibliothèque, en constitue la pièce maîtresse.

El nuevo edificio de la biblioteca central de la Humboldt-Universität, construido en 2009, destaca por sus dimensiones. En su diseño, de inspiración moderna, Max Dudler ha conseguido combinar la biblioteca, que alberga 2,5 millones de volúmenes, con diversas salas de trabajo, una cafetería, un auditorio y las salas centrales de ordenadores y medios. El núcleo del edificio lo constituyen las terrazas que conforman la sala de lectura, que se extienden por las cinco plantas de consulta libre y reciben la luz de un inmenso techo acristalado.

COLLEGIUM HUNGARICUM BERLIN

Dorotheenstraße 12 // Mitte
Tel.: +49 (0)30 2 12 34 00
www.hungaricum.de

Daily 10 am to 7 pm
U6, S1, S2, S3, S5, S7, S25, S75 Friedrichstraße

Erected on the former site of the first Hungarian Cultural Institute of 1924, the building by Schweger Associated Architects—opened in 2007—looks like a modern interpretation of the Bauhaus style. On its six floors are guest apartments, a library, seminar rooms, and the Moholy-Nagy gallery. The heart of the building is the glassed-in panorama room—used for lectures, conferences, concerts, film screenings, and readings—and the media facade.

Auf dem ehemaligen Gelände des ersten ungarischen Kulturinstituts von 1924 eröffnete 2007 der Neubau von Schweger Associated Architects, der an eine moderne Interpretation des Bauhausstils erinnert. Auf sechs Etagen sind Gästewohnungen, Büros, eine Bibliothek, Seminarräume und die Moholy-Nagy-Galerie untergebracht. Herzstücke sind der vollständig verglaste Panoramasaal, der für Vorträge, Tagungen, Konzerte, Filmvorführungen und Lesungen genutzt wird, sowie die Medienfassade.

Le nouvel édifice, conçu par le cabinet Schweger Associated Architects sur l'ancien site du centre culturel hongrois de 1924, a rouvert ses portes en 2007 et une interprétation moderne du courant Bauhaus. Il abrite sur ses six étages des appartements, des bureaux, bibliothèque, des salles de séminaires et la galerie Moholy-Nagy. La salle panoramique vitrée, réservée aux conférences, congrès, concerts, projections de films et aux lectures, et la façade-média constituent les pièces maîtresses de l'édifice.

Sobre el terreno ocupado desde 1924 por el primer instituto cultural húngaro se inauguró en 2007 el edificio diseñado por Schweger Associated Architects, una moderna interpretación del estilo Bauhaus. Sus seis plantas albergan viviendas para visitantes, oficinas, biblioteca, aulas y la galería Moholy-Nagy. El corazón del edificio lo forman la sala panorámica acristalada, en la que se organizan conferencias, seminarios, conciertos y proyecciones, y la fachada mediática.

DEUTSCHES HISTORISCHES MUSEUM

Unter den Linden 2 // Mitte
Tel.: +49 (0)30 20 30 44 44
www.dhm.de

Daily 10 am to 6 pm
U6, S1, S2, S3, S5, S7, S25, S75 Friedrichstraße,
S3, S5, S7, S75 Hackescher Markt

The Chinese-American architect I.M. Pei's new four-floored construction, which was completed in 2004, is the setting for the special exhibitions at the Deutsches Historisches Museum. The building's curved facade with its glass stair tower and the entirely glass-paned foyer with multiple fields of view fit perfectly into its historical surroundings. In the adjoining baroque armoury the DHM presents its permanent exhibition about German history in a European context.

Der Neubau des chinesisch-amerikanischen Architekten I.M.Pei, 2004 vollendet, dient mit vier Ebenen der Präsentation der Sonderausstellungen des Deutschen Historischen Museums. Die geschwungene Fassade des Gebäudes mit dem gläsernen Treppenturm, das vollständig verglaste Foyer mit den verschiedenen Sichtachsen fügen sich perfekt in die historische Umgebung ein. Im angrenzenden barocken Zeughaus präsentiert das DHM seine ständige Ausstellung zur deutschen Geschichte im europäischen Kontext.

Le nouvel édifice, pensé par l'architecte sino-américain I. M. Pei et achevé en 2004, accueille les expositions temporaires du DHM sur quatre niveaux. Sa façade convexe dotée d'une cage d'escalier en verre et son foyer entièrement recouvert d'une verrière dévoilant différents axes de vue s'accordent parfaitement au style plus ancien du quartier. À l'arsenal (Zeughaus), bâtiment baroque adjacent, le DHM présente son exposition permanente sur l'histoire allemande dans le contexte européen.

El edificio diseñado por el arquitecto sinoamericano I. M. Pei y completado en 2004 acoge en sus cuatro plantas las exposiciones especiales organizadas por el DHM. La sinuosa fachada del edificio y la torre acristalada de la escalera, así como las diferentes líneas perspectivas que abre el recibidor vidriado, se integran a la perfección en su histórico entorno. En el vecino edificio barroco del arsenal, el museo alberga su colección permanente, centrada en la historia alemana en el contexto europeo.

A

To Rem Koolhaas, his exposed concrete, aluminum and glass structure—opened in 2003—is a symbol of both Dutch openness and conventional civil service security. A free-standing cube is framed by an L-shaped building that contains living quarters and completes the city block. From the entry, a hallway known as the "trajectory" spirals through the cube via the library, meeting rooms, fitness area, and restaurant, and terminates at the roof garden.

Rem Koolhaas symbolisiert in dem 2003 eröffneten Bauwerk aus Sichtbeton, Aluminium und Glas gleichermaßen holländische Offenheit wie auch die Wahrung der Sicherheit. Ein freistehender Kubus wird von einem L-förmigen Gebäude umrahmt, in dem Wohneinheiten untergebracht sind und der den Blockrand beschließt. Beginnend am Eingang zieht sich ein „Trajekt" genannter Gang, der Bibliothek, Besprechungsräume, Fitnessbereich, Restaurant und Dachterrasse miteinander verbindet, spiralförmig durch den Kubus.

Ce bâtiment alliant le béton apparent, l'aluminium et le verre, conçu par l'architecte Rem Koolhaas, fut inauguré en 2003 et symbolise la transparence hollandaise tout en véhiculant une impression de sécurité. L'édifice de forme cubique est entouré d'une construction en forme de L où sont aménagés des logements pour les invités. La structure interne est traversée d'un long couloir en spirale qui mène à une bibliothèque, des salles de conférences, une salle de sport, un restaurant et une terrasse sur le toit.

Rem Koolhaas refleja en esta construcción de hormigón visto, aluminio y vidrio erigida en 2003 a un tiempo la cordialidad holandesa y la preservación de la seguridad. Un edificio en forma de L enmarca un cubo autónomo en el que se han integrado viviendas y que completa el recuadro exterior. Desde la entrada avanza un pasillo en espiral por todo el cubo que enlaza la biblioteca, las salas conferencias, el gimnasio, el restaurante y la azotea.

NIEDERLÄNDISCHE BOTSCHAFT

Klosterstraße 50 // Mitte
Tel.: +49 (0)30 20 95 64 30
bln.niederlandeweb.de

Mon–Fri 9 am to 1 pm
U2 Klosterstraße

A

Outside, the Neo-Baroque Neuer Marstall at the Schlossplatz looks as opulent as ever. Inside, where imperial grooms were once charged with the care of around 300 horses and coaches, music students now practice in state-of-the-art, soundproof rooms. While preserving the spatial dimensions of this listed building, Anderhalten Architekten designed an interior structure with three concert halls and over 100 practice rooms, all equipped with the latest acoustic technology.

Von seiner äußeren Pracht hat der neobarocke Neue Marstall am Schlossplatz nichts verloren. Im Inneren, wo sich einst kaiserliche Bedienstete um 300 Pferde und Kutschen kümmerten, proben heute Musikstudenten in modernsten schalldichten Räumen. Unter Wahrung der Raumdimensionen des denkmalgeschützten Gebäudes gestalteten Anderhalten Architekten eine Innenstruktur mit drei Konzertsälen und mehr als 100 Proberäumen, die über neuste Akustiktechnik verfügen.

Le Neuer Marstall de style néo-baroque n'a rien perdu de sa magnificence d'antan. Ce lieu, où des serviteurs de l'empereur s'occupaient de 300 chevaux et carrosses à l'époque, abrite de nos jours plusieurs salles modernes insonorisées, où s'exercent des étudiants du conservatoire. Tout en préservant la dimension des pièces de ce monument classé historique, Anderhalten Architekten ont aménagé trois salles de concert et plus de 100 salles de répétition, qui disposent d'installations acoustiques des plus modernes.

El neobarroco Neuer Marstall no ha perdido un ápice de opulencia en su aspecto exterior. En el interior de las antiguas caballerizas imperiales, que en otra época albergaron 300 caballos y carrozas, los estudiantes de música practican en la actualidad en modernas salas insonorizadas. Respetando siempre las dimensiones espaciales del edificio, declarado bien cultural, Anderhalten Architekten creó una estructura interna con tres salas de conciertos y más de 100 salas de ensayo dotadas de la más moderna técnica acústica.

HOCHSCHULE FÜR MUSIK HANNS EISLER

Schlossplatz 7 // Mitte
Tel.: +49 (0)30 6 88 30 52 00
www.hfm-berlin.de

U2 Hausvogteiplatz

A

With their Miniloft, architect/owners Britta Jürgens and Matthew Griffin have designed a brand-new prize-winning hotel concept. By joining a new stainless steel, organically-shaped structure with a restored turn-of-the-century building, they've created a single unit that accommodates 14 minimalistic one-room apartments measuring 325 to 540 sq. ft. each. The architects pay particular attention to sustainability, from a consistent use of renewable energy to ecological cleaning products.

Die Architekten und Inhaber Britta Jürgens und Matthew Griffin haben mit ihrem Haus ein neues, preisgekröntes Hotelkonzept entworfen. Ein organisch geformter Neubau aus Edelstahl wurde mit einem sanierten Bau der Jahrhundertwende zu einer Einheit verbunden und beherbergt 14 minimalistische Einraumappartments zwischen 30 bis 50 m². Besonderes Augenmerk legten die Architekten auf Nachhaltigkeit, angefangen bei der konsequenten Nutzung erneuerbarer Energien bis hin zu ökologischen Reinigungsmitteln.

Les propriétaires, Britta Jürgens et Matthew Griffin, sont également les architectes ayant conçu et transformé leur maison en cet hôtel design qui a remporté plusieurs prix. Cet édifice, de forme organique en acier, est une interaction entre une construction moderne et un immeuble ancien rénové au tournant du siècle passé, qui abrite 14 appartements minimalistes d'une surface de 30 à 50 m². Les architectes ont mis particulièrement l'accent sur la durabilité en optant pour les énergies renouvelables et des détergents écologiques.

Britta Jürgens y Matthew Griffin, propietarios y arquitectos del establecimiento, han creado en éste un nuevo concepto de hotel que les ha valido diversos premios. El edificio, de orgánicas formas en acero inoxidable, se integra en otra construcción rehabilitada de comienzos del siglo XX que alberga 14 apartamentos minimalistas de una habitación, de entre 30 y 50 m². Sus creadores prestaron especial atención a la sostenibilidad, desde el recurso consecuente a energías renovables hasta el uso de productos ecológicos de limpieza.

MINI LOFT

Hessische Straße 5 // Mitte
Tel.: +49 (0)30 8 47 10 90
www.miniloft.com

Mon–Fri 9 am to 1 pm + 2 pm to 6 pm
U6 Naturkundemuseum

BAND DES BUNDES

For the seat of the German government, architects Axel Schultes and Charlotte Frank developed an overall design intended to symbolically unite the formerly divided city. In the location of the historic Embassy Row that was completely destroyed during the war, there is now a campus of buildings consisting of the chancellery by Schultes and Frank, Paul-Löbe- and Marie-Elisabeth Lüders-Haus by Stephan Braunfels and the German parliament by Lord Norman Foster with its distinctive accessible glass dome atop the plenary chamber.

Für den deutschen Regierungssitz entwickelten die Architekten Axel Schultes und Charlotte Frank ein Gesamtkonzept, das die ehemals geteilte Stadt symbolisch verbinden soll. Auf dem Areal des im Krieg vollständig zerstörten Botschaftsquartiers erstreckt sich heute der Band des Bundes genannte Gebäudepark, bestehend aus dem Bundeskanzleramt von Schultes und Frank, Paul-Löbe- und Marie-Elisabeth-Lüders-Haus von Stephan Braunfels und dem Deutschen Bundestag von Lord Norman Foster mit seiner markanten begehbaren Glaskuppel über dem Plenarsaal.

Les architectes Axel Schultes et Charlotte Frank ont mis sur pied un concept architectural pour le siège du gouvernement, symbolisant la réunification de cette ville autrefois divisée. Ce parc d'immeubles s'étend sur l'ensemble de l'ancien quartier des ambassades, qui fut entièrement détruit pendant la guerre. Il se compose de la chancellerie fédérale, de Schultes et Frank, de la maison Paul-Löbe, de la maison Marie-Elisabeth-Lüders, conçues par Stephan Braunfels et du Bundestag, de Lord Norman Foster, avec son imposante coupole de verre qui surplombe la salle plénière.

Para la sede del gobierno alemán, los arquitectos Axel Schultes y Charlotte Frank procuraron vincular simbólicamente la ciudad otrora dividida. En el antiguo barrio de las embajadas se levanta en la actualidad un conjunto de edificios, el Band des Bundes, que incluye la cancillería, la casa Paul-Löbe y Marie-Elisabeth-Lüders, obra de Stephan Braunfels, y el parlamento de Lord Norman Foster, cuya inconfundible cúpula vidriada se eleva sobre la sala de plenos.

BUNDESKANZLERAMT

Willy-Brandt-Straße 1 // Tiergarten
Tel.: +49 (0)30 4 00 00
www.bundesregierung.de

U55 Bundestag

BUNDESTAG

Platz der Republik 1 // Tiergarten
Tel.: +49 (0)30 22 70
www.bundestag.de

U55 Bundestag

PAUL-LÖBE-HAUS

Konrad-Adenauer-Straße // Tiergarten
Tel.: +49 (0)30 22 70
www.bundestag.de

U55 Bundestag

With the 2005 opening of the new building by architects Behnisch & Partner and Werner Durth on Pariser Platz, the Academy—reestablished in 1993—obtained a proper headquarters. Behind an all-glass facade are offices, spaces for events, and several open levels interconnected by a network of free-floating stairways. The Academy hosts a broad spectrum of cultural events, including exhibitions, concerts, readings, dance performances, and film screenings, and awards the annual Berlin Art Prize.

Mit dem 2005 eröffneten Neubau von Behnisch & Partner mit Werner Durth am Pariser Platz hat die 1993 wiedervereinte Akademie einen repräsentativen Hauptsitz erhalten. Hinter einer vollständig verglasten Fassade befinden sich Büros, Veranstaltungsräume und mehrere offene Ebenen, die freischwebende Treppen miteinander verbinden. Die Akademie bietet ein breites Spektrum an kulturellen Veranstaltungen, darunter Ausstellungen, Konzerte, Lesungen, Tanz- und Filmvorführungen und verleiht jährlich den Berliner Kunstpreis.

Depuis 2005, le siège de l'Académie, à nouveau réunie en 1993, se situe au sein d'un nouvel édifice en bordure de la Pariser Platz, conçu par les architectes Behnisch & Partner et Werner Durth. Derrière la façade vitrée, on trouve des bureaux, des salles de conférences et des espaces ouverts, reliés par des escaliers suspendus. L'Académie propose divers événements culturels dont des expositions, des concerts et des lectures. Elle organise également la cérémonie de remise du prix des Arts de la Ville de Berlin.

En el edificio diseñado por Behnisch & Partner junto con Werner Durth e inaugurado en Pariser Platz en 2005, la reunificada Academia ha encontrado una sede central a su medida. Tras la fachada, totalmente acristalada, se encuentran oficinas, salas de actos y diversas superficies abiertas conectadas por medio de escaleras autoportantes. La Academia ofrece un amplio abanico de eventos culturales: exposiciones, conciertos, ponencias... sin olvidar la concesión anual del Premio de las Artes de Berlín.

AKADEMIE DER KÜNSTE

Pariser Platz 4 // Mitte
Tel.: +49 (0)30 2 00 57 10 00
www.adk.de

Tue–Sun 11 am to 8 pm during events
U55, S1, S2, S25 Brandenburger Tor

DENKMAL FÜR DIE
ERMORDETEN JUDEN EUROPAS

Cora-Berliner-Straße 1 // Mitte
Tel.: +49 (0)30 26 39 43 11
www.stiftung-denkmal.de

Field of Stelae: 24 h, Information Center: Apr–Sep 10 am to 8 pm,
Oct–Mar 10 am to 7 pm
U55, S1, S2, S25 Brandenburger Tor

The Holocaust Memorial, designed by Peter Eisenman and opened in 2005, consists of 2,711 off-kilter concrete blocks of varying heights. Occupying a prominent spot in the city's center, the memorial is an island of calm intended to inspire reflection and its vast expanse of approximately 4.7 acres is a monument to memory. An underground information center serves as a museum for the complex and gives faces to the victims.

2 711 unterschiedlich hohe Betonstelen, keine davon gerade, bilden das von Peter Eisenman entworfene und 2005 eröffnete Holocaustmahnmal. An einer prominenten Stelle mitten in der Stadt ist das Feld ein Ort der Ruhe, der zum Nachdenken anregen will und mit seiner enormen Fläche von ca. 19 000 m² ein Zeichen der Erinnerung setzt. Ein unter-irdisch angelegter Ort der Information ergänzt den Komplex als Museum und gibt den Opfern ein Gesicht.

Composé de 2 711 stèles en béton de hau-teurs différentes, le Mémorial aux victimes de l'Holocauste, conçu par l'architecte Peter Eisenman, fut inauguré en 2005. Construit sur un site éminent dans le centre de la ville et réparti sur une surface d'environ 19 000 m², le Mémorial est un lieu de recueillement et de mémoire. Le centre de documentation, situé dans le sous-sol du champ des stèles, a pour vo-cation d'informer les visiteurs sur l'Holo-causte et de mettre un visage sur les noms des victimes.

2 711 estelas de hormigón de distin-tas alturas, ninguna de ellas paralela, constituyen el monumento diseñado en 1999 por Peter Eisenman e inaugurado en 2005. La explanada, situada en un espacio prominente del centro de Berlín, es un oasis de tranquilidad que invita a la reflexión y el recuerdo en sus cerca de 19 000 m². Un espacio subterráneo de información completa el complejo museístico y pone rostro a las víctimas.

A

Otto Bock

DISCOVER

SCIENCE CENTER MEDIZINTECHNIK

A futuristic facade modeled on the structure of muscle fibers already hints at what can be found inside this building between Potsdamer Platz and the Brandenburg Gate, first opened in 2009. A multimedia exhibit explains "what moves us." Designed by Gnädiger Architekten, the center's organic structures and cutting-edge interior successfully blend contemporary architecture and state-of-the-art technology. The facade is partially illuminated by a light installation.

Der Struktur von Muskelfasern nachempfunden, lässt die futuristisch anmutende Fassade des 2009 eröffneten Gebäudes zwischen Potsdamer Platz und Brandenburger Tor schon vermuten, was sich im Inneren befindet. Die multimediale Ausstellung des Hauses erläutert, „was uns bewegt". Das von Gnädiger Architekten entworfene Center mit seinen organischen Strukturen und modernstem Interieur ist eine gelungene Verbindung von zeitgenössischer Baukunst und neuester Technik. Eine Lichtinstallation erhellt Teile der Fassade.

La façade futuriste de cet édifice, inauguré en 2009 et situé entre la Potsdamer Platz et la porte de Brandebourg, est inspirée de la structure des fibres musculaires de l'être humain et laisse présager au visiteur ce qu'il découvrira à l'intérieur. L'exposition interactive nous aide à comprendre « ce qui nous motorise ». Cet édifice aux structures organiques, conçu par Gnädiger Architekten, est une interaction entre l'architecture contemporaine et la technique moderne. Une installation d'éclairage illumine un pan de façade.

Inspirada en las fibras musculares, la futurista fachada del edificio inaugurado en 2009 entre Potsdamer Platz y la puerta de Brandenburgo da una idea de lo que espera al visitante en su interior. La exposición multimedia que allí se presenta lleva por título "lo que nos mueve". El centro, diseñado por Gnädiger Architekten, cuenta con una estructura orgánica y un modernísimo interior que vinculan a la perfección la arquitectura contemporánea con las técnicas más novedosas. Un sistema de luces ilumina parte de la fachada.

SCIENCE CENTER MEDIZINTECHNIK

Ebertstraße 15a // Mitte
Tel.: +49 (0)30 3 98 20 60
www.sciencecenter-medizintechnik.de

Thu–Sun 10 am to 6 pm
U2, S1, S2, S25 Potsdamer Platz

A

This landmarked 1880s power station's main claim to fame is its earlier use as a techno club. After the club closed in 1997, the building was completely refurbished by the Berlin architectural firm HSH. In 2005, the E-Werk was reopened as an urban center with offices, apartment buildings and event spaces. The vintage building was crowned with a modern roof garden, for a total of 27,000 sq. ft. of space available for events, concerts and receptions.

Bekanntheit erlangte das denkmalgeschützte Umspannwerk aus den 1880er Jahren vor allem durch seine Nutzung als Technoclub. Nach der Schließung des Clubs 1997 erfolgte eine umfassende Sanierung durch das Berliner Architekturbüro HSH. 2005 eröffnete das E-Werk neu als Ort urbanen Lebens mit Büros, Wohnhäusern und großen Veranstaltungsräumen. Der Altbau wurde durch eine moderne Dachterrasse erweitert, die zusammen mit den Hallen auf einer Fläche von rund 2 500 m² Platz für Events, Konzerte und Empfänge bietet.

Ce poste de transformation des années 1880, classé monument historique, doit sa notoriété à son réaménagement en club techno. Après sa fermeture en 1997, l'édifice fut restauré par le cabinet d'architectes HSH. Transformé en lieu de vie urbaine et inauguré en 2005, il abrite des bureaux, des habitations et des salles de conférences. Cet immeuble ancien, avec son toit réaménagé en terrasse moderne et ses diverses salles, s'étend sur 2 500 m² et est devenu un lieu approprié pour l'organisation d'événements, de concerts et de réceptions.

La fama le llegó a esta antigua subestación eléctrica de finales del siglo XIX como club de música tecno. Tras el cierre del local en 1997 se llevó a cabo una profunda renovación, dirigida por el despacho berlinés de arquitectos HSH. En 2005, E-Werk abrió de nuevo sus puertas como espacio urbano con oficinas, bloques de viviendas y amplias salas de actos. El antiguo edificio se ha visto ampliado con una moderna azotea que, junto con las distintas salas, ofrece cerca de 2 500 m² para eventos, conciertos y recepciones.

E-WERK

Mauerstraße 78–80 // Mitte
Tel.: +49 (0)30 2 00 75 60
www.ewerk.net

By appointment
U2, U6 Stadtmitte

HSH

Hoyer
Schindele
Hirschmüller

Few architecture firms in Berlin have caused as much of a stir in recent years as HSH. The three architects after which it is named—Florian Hoyer, Harald Schindele and Markus Hirschmüller—are masters at integrating new architecture into the existing urban environment. Their building designs are based almost exclusively on the specific characteristics of existing materials and thus tell a new story that builds on the old. Their projects, called case studies, always reflect the context of their surroundings. For example, they use the "airspace" of fire department access routes or take advantage of narrow plots between buildings to add new elements to the original architecture. Many of their creations look like real-life manifestations from the classic computer game Tetris applied to urban spaces. Thanks to their experience renovating old buildings, they have been able to transform the closed, autonomous character of the E-Werk into a bright, modern office building. In 2009 they converted another Berlin landmark, Café Moskau, that radiates a new glow ever since.

Nur wenige Architekturbüros in Berlin haben in den letzten Jahren so viel Furore gemacht wie HSH – die drei Namensgeber Florian Hoyer, Harald Schindele und Markus Hirschmüller schaffen es glänzend, neue Architektur in die bestehenden stadträumlichen Gegebenheiten zu integrieren. Sie bauen fast ausschließlich unter Berücksichtigung der spezifischen Eigenarten der vorhandenen Substanz und erzählen so eine neue Geschichte auf der Grundlage des bereits Bestehenden. So reflektieren ihre Case Study genannten Projekte immer den Kontext der Umgebung. Sie nutzen dabei zum Beispiel den „Luftraum" von Feuerwehrzufahrten oder stellen sich der Herausforderung schmaler Baulücken, um ursprüngliche Architektur mit neuen Elementen zu ergänzen. Manche ihrer Kreationen wirken dabei wie Realität gewordene Manifestationen des Computerspielklassikers Tetris – eingesetzt in den urbanen Raum. Mit ihren Erfahrungen im Umgang mit alter Bausubstanz konnten sie den geschlossenen und autonomen Charakter des E-Werks in ein lichtes, modernes Bürogebäude verwandeln. 2009 haben sie mit dem Café Moskau ein weiteres Berliner Wahrzeichen umgebaut, das seitdem in neuem Glanz erstrahlt.

Peu de cabinets d'architectes ont fait fureur dans le monde de l'architecture comme HSH, dont les trois associés, Florian Hoyer, Harald Schindele et Markus Hirschmüller, ont su parfaitement intégrer leur style au contexte architectural des alentours. Ils adaptent leurs créations exclusivement aux spécificités de chaque substance donnée et remodèlent ainsi l'histoire de chaque bâtiment à leur manière. Chacun de leurs projets, également appelés « case study », reflète toujours le contexte des alentours. Ils utilisent, par exemple, l'espace « aérien » des accès des stations de pompiers ou des terrains vagues non utilisés pour y insérer de nouveaux éléments de manière à compléter l'architecture d'origine. Certaines de leurs créations rappellent le principe du jeu Tetris, mais appliqué au monde réel urbain. Grâce à leur expérience des constructions anciennes, ils ont transformé le caractère austère et autonome de l'E-Werk en un immeuble de bureaux lumineux et moderne. Lors de la rénovation en 2009 d'un autre emblème de la capitale, ils ont su rendre au Café Moskau toute sa splendeur d'antan.

Pocos despachos de arquitectura berlinesa han levantado tantas pasiones en los últimos años como HSH: los tres socios Florian Hoyer, Harald Schindele y Markus Hirschmüller consiguen como ningún otro profesional integrar la nueva arquitectura en los espacios arquitectónicos que se ponen a su disposición. Trabajan casi exclusivamente desde el respeto de las características específicas de la estructura original y consiguen de ese modo narrar una nueva historia sobre la base de lo ya existente. De ahí que sus proyectos, sus case studies, reflejen siempre el contexto de su entorno. Así, por ejemplo, aprovechan el "espacio aéreo" de los accesos de vehículos de bomberos y el reto que suponen los huecos reducidos para complementar la arquitectura original con nuevos elementos. Algunas de sus creaciones se antojan la materialización física del Tetris, título clásico de los videojuegos, en el contexto urbano. Gracias a su experiencia en el trabajo con estructuras antiguas han conseguido transformar el carácter cerrado y autónomo del E-Werk en un luminoso y moderno edificio de oficinas. En 2009 reacondicionaron otro local emblemático de Berlín, el Café Moskau, que desde entonces brilla con una nueva luz.

TOPOGRAPHIE DES TERRORS

Niederkirchnerstraße 8 // Kreuzberg
Tel.: +49 (0)30 25 45 09 50
www.topographie.de

Daily 10 am to 8 pm
U6 Kochstraße

During the Third Reich, this was the site of premises shared by Gestapo Headquarters, and the SS High Command, and the Reich Security Main Office—the main proponents of Nazi terror. Today, only cellar walls remain. After years of controversy around the original design by Peter Zumthor, the 8,600-sq.-ft. exhibition and documentation center, which was designed by Ursula Wilms and also houses the foundation and a library, finally opened in 2010.

Während des Dritten Reichs waren auf dem Gelände die Zentralen der Geheimen Staatspolizei, der SS-Führung und des Reichssicherheitshauptamtes vereint – die Hauptträger des NS-Terrors –, von denen nur Kellermauern erhalten geblieben sind. Nach jahrelangen Kontroversen um den ursprünglichen Bauentwurf von Peter Zumthor konnte 2010 das 800 m² große, von Ursula Wilms entworfene Ausstellungs- und Dokumentationszentrum eröffnet werden, in dem auch die Stiftung und eine Bibliothek untergebracht sind.

Ce site abritait à l'époque les institutions centrales de l'appareil de persécution et de terreur du régime nazi, comme la Gestapo, la direction SS et l'Office Central de la Sécurité du Reich. De nos jours, il ne reste que les fondements de l'ancien bâtiment. La conception initiale de Peter Zumthor fut longtemps controversée. L'édifice actuel, d'une dimension de 800 m², fut finalement inauguré en 2010 avec l'ouverture du centre d'exposition et de documentation de l'architecte Ursula Wilms, qui abrite une fondation et une bibliothèque.

Durante el Tercer Reich, sobre este terreno se alzaban las sedes centrales de la policía secreta del estado, la dirección de las SS y los servicios de seguridad del Reich; en la actualidad, sólo perviven los muros de los sótanos. Tras años de discusiones en torno al proyecto original de Peter Zumthor, en 2010 pudieron al fin inaugurarse los 800 m² del centro de exposiciones y documentación concebido por Ursula Wilms, que alberga también la fundación y una biblioteca.

A

JÜDISCHES MUSEUM BERLIN

JÜDISCHES MUSEUM BERLIN

Lindenstraße 9–14 // Kreuzberg
Tel.: +49 (0)30 25 99 33 00
www.jmberlin.de

Mon 10 am to 10 pm, Tue–Sun 10 am to 8 pm
U1, U6 Hallesches Tor

Architect Daniel Libeskind describes his concept for the Jewish Museum completed in 1998 as "Between the Lines." Intersecting axes and lines dominate both the contours and the interior of this deconstructivist building and represent the continuities and breaks in German-Jewish history. Instead of normal windows, the almost entirely closed zinc facade is pierced by narrow slits. Entrance is via the old Baroque museum building with the new glass courtyard by Libeskind.

„Between the Lines" nennt Architekt Daniel Libeskind seinen Entwurf für den 1998 vollendeten Neubau des Jüdischen Museums Berlin. Sich kreuzende Achsen und Linien dominieren sowohl den Grundriss als auch das Innere des dekonstruktivistischen Gebäudes und stehen für die Kontinuitäten und Brüche deutschjüdischer Geschichte. Statt normaler Fenster durchbrechen schmale Schlitze die fast geschlossene Zinkfassade. Der Zutritt erfolgt über den barocken Altbau mit dem neuen Glashof von Libeskind.

Projet intitulé « Between the Lines », le nouveau Musée juif de l'architecte Daniel Libeskind fut inauguré en 1998. Cet édifice, pur produit du déconstructivisme, tout en brisures, zigzags et arêtes, est un rappel saisissant à l'histoire judéo-allemande. La façade extérieure en zinc demeure aveugle, même si elle compte une multitude de fenêtres, plutôt considérées comme des meurtrières. L'entrée se situe dans le bâtiment de style baroque et se poursuit dans la cour vitrée intérieure, autre chef-d'œuvre de Libeskind.

Daniel Libeskind tituló "Between the Lines" su proyecto para el nuevo edificio del Museo Judío, completado en 1998. Ejes y líneas entrecruzadas dominan tanto el plano como los interiores de este edificio deconstructivista y simbolizan los hilos continuistas y las interrupciones de la historia judía en Alemania. Estrechas ranuras sustituyen las ventanas tradicionales en la casi estanca fachada de zinc. Se accede al edificio a través de un viejo edificio barroco al que Libeskind dotó de un nuevo patio vidriado.

In addition to a large and a small arena, the tent-like concrete roof of the Tempodrom designed by Meinhard von Gerkan also conceals a wellness pool. Visitors can avail themselves of several saunas and steam baths, as well as a traditional open-air Japanese onsen bath, a bar, and a restaurant. The centerpiece is the darkened dome with a circular saltwater pool where soft music is piped in through underwater speakers.

Unter dem zeltartigen Betondach des von Meinhard von Gerkan geplanten Tempodroms befindet sich neben der großen und einer kleineren Arena auch ein Wellnessbad. Mehrere Saunen und Dampfbäder, ein traditionelles japanisches Onsen-Bad im Außenbereich sowie eine Bar und ein Restaurant stehen dem Besucher zur Verfügung. Das Herzstück bildet ein abgedunkelter Kuppelraum mit einem kreisrunden Solebecken, das über Unterwasserlautsprecher sanfte Musik verströmt.

Surplombé d'un toit en béton en forme de chapiteau, le Tempodrom de l'architecte Meinhard von Gerkan abrite deux arènes et un complexe thermal. Le visiteur pourra se détendre dans les divers saunas et bains turcs, les sources japonaises situés à l'extérieur ainsi que savourer un repas au restaurant et un verre au bar. La coupole, pièce maîtresse de l'édifice, abrite un bassin circulaire d'eau saline où le visiteur se laissera bercer dans une ambiance tamisée au rythme d'une musique douce, diffusée par des haut-parleurs sous la surface de l'eau.

Bajo la carpa de hormigón del Tempodrom diseñado por Meinhard von Gerkan, podemos encontrar un balneario, además de un gran escenario y otro de menores dimensiones. Diversas saunas y baños de vapor, un tradicional baño onsen japonés en la zona exterior así como un bar y un restaurante están a disposición de los bañistas. En el centro del complejo, una sala abovedada en semipenumbra con una piscina redonda de agua salada en la que relajantes melodías emanan de los altavoces instalados bajo el agua.

LIQUIDROM

Möckernstraße 10 // Kreuzberg
Tel.: +49 (0)30 2 58 00 78 20
www.liquidrom-berlin.de

Sun–Thu 10 am to midnight, Fri+Sat 10 am to 1 am
U1, U7 Möckernbrücke

BAUHAUS-ARCHIV BERLIN

Klingelhöferstraße 14 // Tiergarten
Tel.: +49 (0)30 2 54 00 20
www.bauhaus.de

Museum: Wed–Mon 10 am to 5 pm
U1, U2, U3, U4 Nollendorfplatz

This building was designed by former Bauhaus director Walter Gropius and built between 1976–1979. Its distinctive silhouette has made it a Berlin landmark. With an extensive permanent collection and numerous temporary exhibitions, the archive and museum make an important contribution to research and the presentation of the history and impact of the architecture, design and art of Bauhaus, its students and its descendants.

Vom ehemaligen Bauhausdirektor Walter Gropius geplant, wurde das Gebäude in den Jahren 1976–79 errichtet. Aufgrund seiner markanten Silhouette ist es zu einem Wahrzeichen der Stadt geworden. Archiv und Museum tragen mittels der umfangreichen ständigen Sammlung und wechselnden Ausstellungen zur Erforschung und Präsentation der Geschichte und Wirkung von Architektur, Design und Kunst des Bauhauses, seiner Schüler und Nachfolger bei.

Le Bauhaus Archiv fut construit entre 1976 et 1979 d'après les plans initiaux du fondateur du Bauhaus, Walter Gropius. Sa silhouette, qui ne laisse pas indifférent, est la raison pour laquelle ce bâtiment est devenu un des emblèmes de la capitale. La vocation des archives et du musée, à travers l'importante collection permanente et les expositions temporaires, est de faire découvrir à ses élèves et successeurs l'histoire et la contribution artistique du courant artistique Bauhaus dans l'architecture, l'art et le design.

Concebido por Walter Gropius, antiguo director de la Bauhaus, el edificio fue construido entre 1976 y 1979. Su característica silueta lo ha convertido en una de las señas de identidad de la ciudad. Gracias a su extensa colección permanente y a las distintas exposiciones que en ellos se organizan, el archivo y el museo suponen una importante contribución al estudio y presentación de la historia y el influjo de la arquitectura, diseño y arte de la Bauhaus, sus discipulos y sus sucesores.

A

PHILOLOGISCHE BIBLIOTHEK

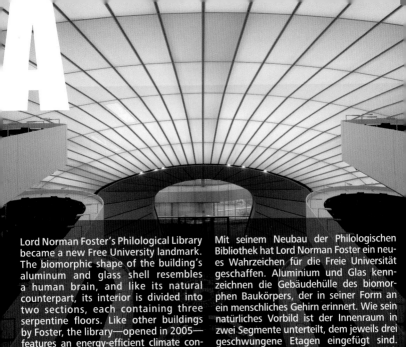

A

Lord Norman Foster's Philological Library became a new Free University landmark. The biomorphic shape of the building's aluminum and glass shell resembles a human brain, and like its natural counterpart, its interior is divided into two sections, each containing three serpentine floors. Like other buildings by Foster, the library—opened in 2005—features an energy-efficient climate control concept.

Mit seinem Neubau der Philologischen Bibliothek hat Lord Norman Foster ein neues Wahrzeichen für die Freie Universität geschaffen. Aluminium und Glas kennzeichnen die Gebäudehülle des biomorphen Baukörpers, der in seiner Form an ein menschliches Gehirn erinnert. Wie sein natürliches Vorbild ist der Innenraum in zwei Segmente unterteilt, dem jeweils drei geschwungene Etagen eingefügt sind. Wie andere Bauten Fosters zeichnet sich die 2005 eröffnete Bibliothek durch ihr energieeffizientes Raumklimakonzept aus.

En concevant le nouveau bâtiment de la bibliothèque, Lord Norman Foster a fait de l'Université Libre de Berlin un nouvel emblème de la ville. La façade extérieure, constituée d'aluminium et de verre, caractérise cette construction biomorphique en forme de cerveau humain. Tout comme son modèle morphologique, la structure intérieure est divisée en deux parties, sur chacune desquelles sont répartis trois étages arqués. Comme les autres œuvres de Foster, la bibliothèque, inaugurée en 2005, se distingue par l'efficience énergétique de sa climatisation.

Con el nuevo edificio de la Biblioteca de Filología, Lord Norman Foster ha creado una nueva seña de identidad para la Universidad Libre. El aluminio y el vidrio caracterizan el exterior de la construcción biomorfa, cuyos volúmenes recuerdan el cerebro humano. Al igual que su modelo, el espacio interior está dividido en dos segmentos, compartimentados a su vez en tres curvilíneas plantas. Al igual que otros edificios de Foster, la biblioteca, inaugurada en 2005, destaca por la excelente eficiencia energética de su diseño.

PHILOLOGISCHE BIBLIOTHEK

Habelschwerdter Allee 45 // Dahlem
Tel.: +49 (0)30 83 85 88 88
www.ub.fu-berlin.de

Mon–Fri 9 am to 10 pm, Sat+Sun 10 am to 6 pm
U3 Thielplatz

DESIGN

D

Local history influences the work of designers in Berlin more than almost any other major world metropolis. Over the years, a very independent design scene took shape with almost no connection to local industry, returning only sporadically after the war. Its broad spectrum is seen in a large number of shops and boutiques, at fashion and product design shows like Bread&Butter and DMY, Fashion Week, or other platforms. Many fashion labels and small design firms have made Berlin their home since the city offers the infrastructure and creative environment of a world-class metropolis yet has relatively low housing and living costs. In both fashion and products, "Made in Berlin" design enjoys great popularity due to its characteristic signature. The direct contrast between the charm of former epochs and the sleekness of modernity is a recurring theme of the Berlin style, seen also in interior design, as at Hotel Michelberger.

In kaum einer anderen Weltmetropole beeinflusst die lokale Geschichte die Arbeit der Designer mehr als in Berlin. Fast ohne Verbindung zur örtlichen Industrie, die sich nach dem Krieg nur sporadisch wieder angesiedelt hat, entwickelte sich über die Jahre eine sehr unabhängige Designszene. Diese zeigt ihr großes Spektrum in einer Vielzahl von Shops und Boutiquen, auf Mode- und Produktdesignmessen, wie der Bread&Butter und dem DMY, der Fashion Week oder anderen Plattformen. Zahlreiche Modelabels und kleine Designbüros haben Berlin als ihren Standort gewählt, denn die Stadt bietet die Infrastruktur und das kreative Umfeld einer Weltmetropole bei verhältnismäßig geringen Wohn- und Lebenshaltungskosten. Sowohl bei Mode als auch Produkten, Design „Made in Berlin" erfreut sich wegen seiner typischen Handschrift großer Beliebtheit. Den Charme vergangener Zeiten in unmittelbaren Kontrast zu der schlichten Moderne zu setzen, ist dabei ein immer wiederkehrendes Gestaltungsmotiv des Berliner Stils, das sich, wie beim Hotel Michelberger, auch im Interior Design niederschlägt.

n'y a guère d'autres métropoles mondiales que Berlin pour ressentir autant l'influence de l'histoire locale dans les créations des designers. Un milieu du design particulièrement indépendant se développa au fils des années, en relation quasiment inexistante avec l'industrie locale, qui n'est apparue que sporadiquement après la guerre. Une multitude de magasins et de boutiques, des salons de prêt-à-porter et de design industriel comme le Bread&Butter et le festival DMY, la Fashion Week ou d'autres plateformes, témoignent de l'infinie richesse de cet univers. De nombreux labels de mode et petites agences de design ont choisi Berlin comme lieu d'implantation, la ville disposant de l'infrastructure et de l'environnement propice à toute forme de créativité dignes d'une métropole, tout en offrant une qualité de vie ainsi que des prix de location relativement abordables. Tant en matière de mode que d'accessoires, le design « made in Berlin », dont la griffe est unique, jouit d'une grande popularité. Le contraste flagrant entre le charme des époques passées et la modernité des lignes épurées est un thème de plus en plus récurrent que l'on retrouve dans les créations de style bernois et qui se reflète notamment dans l'architecture d'intérieur, comme par exemple dans la décoration de l'Hotel Michelberger.

No hay en todo el mundo una metrópolis como Berlín en la que la historia local determine hasta tal punto la obra de los diseñadores. Desvinculado casi por completo de la industria, que sólo esporádicamente regresó a la ciudad tras la guerra, con el paso de los años ha ido desarrollándose un mundillo del diseño muy independiente, que se manifiesta en un amplio espectro de tiendas y negocios, muestras de moda y diseño como Bread&Butter y DMY, la Fashion Week u otras plataformas. Diversas casas de moda y pequeños talleres de diseño se han establecido en Berlín, ya que la ciudad ofrece la infraestructura y el entorno creativo de la metrópolis con un coste inmobiliario y de manutención relativamente reducido. Tanto la moda como los productos de diseño "Made in Berlin" gozan de gran aprecio gracias a su sello característico. El contraste entre el encanto de antaño y el escueto estilo moderno es uno de los motivos recurrentes del estilo berlinés, que encuentra también (como en el caso del Hotel Michelberger) reflejo en el diseño de interiores.

ACKSELHAUS & BLUE HOME

Belforter Straße 21 // Prenzlauer Berg
Tel.: +49 (0)30 44 33 76 33
www.ackselhaus.de

U2 Senefelderplatz

Inspired by his extensive travels, Ulf Acksel converted two renovated 19th-century buildings into a special kind of boutique hotel. Each of the 35 rooms and suites has a different theme. Using high-quality materials and with loving attention to detail, Acksel has created intimate microcosms far from the noise of the city. Highlights include a Mediterranean garden in the courtyard and the Club del Mar restaurant.

Inspiriert von seinen zahlreichen Reisen hat Ulf Acksel zwei renovierte Häuser aus der Gründerzeit zu einem Boutique-hotel der besonderen Art umgestaltet. Jedes der 35 Studios und Apartments ist thematisch anders gestaltet. Mit hochwertigen Materialien und viel Liebe zum Detail wurden kleine, intime Welten fernab vom Großstadtlärm geschaffen. Der mediterrane Garten im Innenhof ist ein besonderes Highlight, ebenso das Hausrestaurant Club del Mar.

Inspiré par ses nombreux voyages, Ulf Acksel a restauré deux maisons datant du XIXᵉ siècle et les a transformées en un hôtel-boutique de style unique. L'aménagement des 35 studios et appartements s'articule autour de thématiques différentes. Son choix pour des matériaux de qualité et son amour du détail ont permis de créer l'atmosphère intime de contrées lointaines au vacarme de la ville. Le jardin méditerranéen dans la cour intérieure et le restaurant Club del Mar sont les coups de cœur de ce lieu insolite.

Tomando inspiración de sus frecuentes viajes, Ulf Acksel ha remodelado dos edificios de mediados del siglo XIX para convertirlos en un hotelito lleno de encanto. Cada uno de los 35 estudios y apartamentos ha sido decorado con motivos diferentes. En ellos se han creado pequeños e íntimos mundos alejados del bullicio urbano con nobles materiales y mucha atención al detalle. El jardín mediterráneo del patio interior es uno de sus grandes atractivos, junto con el restaurante Club del Mar del propio establecimiento.

The international private club opened its first German location in the Mitte district in 2010. A former department store was converted into luxury accommodations with 40 rooms, a movie theater, bars, and restaurant, as well as a spa and fitness area. The club is crowned by a rooftop terrace and swimming pool. The interior combines classic opulence with modern elements. Overstuffed furniture, dark wood floors and velvet curtains quote the style of venerable English clubs.

Der internationale Privatclub eröffnete 2010 in Berlin Mitte seine erste Deutschlanddependance. Ein ehemaliges Kaufhaus wurde zu einer Luxusherberge mit 40 Zimmern, einem Kino, Bars und Restaurant sowie einem Spa- und Fitnessbereich umgebaut. Gekrönt wird der Club von einer Dachterrasse mit Pool. Das Interieur verbindet klassische Opulenz mit modernen Elementen. Voluminöse Polstermöbel, dunkle Holzböden und samtene Vorhänge zitieren den Stil altehrwürdiger englischer Clubs.

Ce club privé international a inauguré sa première filière allemande en 2010 dans un ancien grand magasin du centre de Berlin. Cette auberge de luxe abrite aujourd'hui 40 chambres, un cinéma, plusieurs bars, un restaurant ainsi qu'un club de fitness et de bien-être. La terrasse sur le toit avec piscine en constitue la couronne. La décoration allie le style classique opulent au moderne. Les meubles rembourrés, le plancher en bois foncé et les tentures en velours reflètent le style d'honorables clubs anglais.

La red internacional de clubes privados inauguró en 2010 su primera sucursal alemana en Berlín Mitte. Una antigua galería comercial ha pasado a ser un albergue de lujo con 40 habitaciones, un cine, bares y restaurantes, un balneario y un gimnasio. La guinda del pastel la pone la piscina de la azotea. En el interior convive la opulencia clásica con elementos modernos. Pesados muebles tapizados, suelos oscuros de madera y cortinas de terciopelo evocan el estilo de los clubes ingleses.

SOHO HOUSE BERLIN

Torstraße 1 // Mitte
Tel.: +49 (0)30 4 05 04 40
www.sohohouseberlin.com

U2 Rosa-Luxemburg-Platz

Concealed behind an unassuming facade, the interior is a patchwork of luxurious sophistication. The generous lobby features high-quality materials, while rooms and apartments convey a simple, classic hominess. The roof garden, which is catered during the summer months, commands a panoramic view of Berlin's Mitte district. Designed by REM+tec architects and appointed by interior designer Ester Bruzkus, this centrally located hotel is a favorite address for Berlin's style-conscious visitors.

Hinter einer schlichten Fassade verborgen, besticht das Interieur durch ein Patchwork mit luxuriösem Finish. Das Foyer ist großzügig und mit hochwertigen Materialien gestaltet, die Zimmer und Apartments hingegen vermitteln schlichte, edle Wohnlichkeit. Von der im Sommer bewirteten Dachterrasse aus bietet sich ein Panoramablick über Berlin-Mitte. Von REM+tec Architekten geplant und eingerichtet durch die Innenarchitektin Ester Bruzkus, ist das zentral gelegene Hotel eine Topadresse für stilbewusste Berlin-Besucher.'

Camouflé derrière une façade des plus humbles, on se laisse éblouir à l'intérieur par un patchwork aux finitions de luxe. Le foyer d'un luxe abondant, constitué de matériaux de qualité, contraste avec le côté humble et noble des chambres et des appartements. La terrasse sur le toit, avec son restaurant en été, offre une vue panoramique sur le centre de Berlin. Cet hôtel, conçu par les architectes REM+tec et aménagé par l'architecte d'intérieur Ester Bruzkus, est sans conteste une des adresses à ne pas manquer à Berlin.

Oculto tras una anodina fachada, el interior del establecimiento deslumbra con una mezcolanza de estilos que subrayan su lujoso carácter. El espacioso vestíbulo, decorado con los mejores materiales, contrasta con la sobria elegancia de las habitaciones y apartamentos. Desde la azotea, convertida en terraza en los meses estivales, se ofrece una vista panorámica del centro de Berlín. El céntrico hotel, obra de los architector REM+tec et la interiorista Ester Bruzkus, es el alojamiento ideal para quienes quieren visitar Berlín con estilo.

HOTEL AMANO

Auguststraße 43 // Mitte
Tel.: +49 (0)30 8 09 41 50
www.hotel-amano.com

U8 Rosenthaler Platz

Located in the up-and-coming district surrounding the former Spittelmarkt, the Cosmo Hotel fits perfectly into Berlin's cosmopolitan atmosphere. Sleek cubes dominate the modern, urban furnishings, which are juxtaposed with tinges of color and organic shapes, such as the lights by Nik Schweiger. With their ceiling-high windows, the 84 rooms and suites offer views of the colorful life of the city. A concierge service provides guests with insider tips on the hottest clubs, bars and shops.

Im aufstrebenden Stadtviertel um den ehemaligen Spittelmarkt gelegen, passt sich das Cosmo Hotel Berlin in die Großstadtatmosphäre Berlins ein. Glatte kubische Formen dominieren die moderne, urbane Einrichtung, die mit Farbakzenten und organischen Formen wie bei den Leuchten von Nik Schweiger abgerundet wird. Die 84 Zimmer und Suiten bieten mit raumhohen Fenstern Ausblicke auf das bunte Treiben der Stadt. Ein Concierge-Service gibt Gästen Insidertipps zu den angesagtesten Clubs, Bars und Shops.

Situé dans le quartier en pleine expansion aux alentours de l'ancien Spittelmarkt, cet hôtel s'accorde parfaitement avec l'atmosphère de la capitale. Formes cubiques aux accents colorés et aux formes organiques, comme le démontrent les luminaires conçus par Nik Schweiger, confèrent un style moderne à cet édifice urbain. Les 84 chambres et suites sont dotées de hautes fenêtres qui permettent de profiter du tumulte coloré de la ville. Le service des concierges renseigne le visiteur sur les clubs, bars et magasins en vogue à Berlin.

Sito en el pujante barrio que rodea el antiguo Spittelmarkt, el Cosmo Hotel se integra a la perfección en el ambiente cosmopolita de Berlín. Las formas lisas y cúbicas dominan una decoración moderna y urbana matizada por pinceladas de color y formas orgánicas como las de las lámparas de Nik Schweiger. Sus 84 habitaciones y suites ofrecen desde sus enormes ventanales magníficas vistas sobre el bullicio de la ciudad. Los conserjes le recomendarán encantados los mejores bares, tiendas y discotecas.

COSMO HOTEL BERLIN

Spittelmarkt 13 // Mitte
Tel.: +49 (0)30 58 58 22 22
www.cosmo-hotel.de

U2 Spittelmarkt

D

HOTEL MICHELBERGER

D

As an eclectic cross between a design hotel and a youth hostel, the Hotel Michelberger breathes new life into the industry. The design concept of Berlin's studio aisslinger blends into the loft structure of the old industrial building in an innovative patchwork. The 119 single, double, triple, and quad rooms each have their own theme and can sleep up to ten people. A unique feature is the courtyard stage for concerts and other events.

Mit seinem eklektischen Mix aus Designhotel und Jugendherberge bringt das Hotel Michelberger neuen Wind in die Branche. Das Designkonzept des Berliner studio aisslinger fügt sich als innovatives Patchwork in die Loftstruktur des alten Industriegebäudes ein. Die 119 Einzel- und Mehrbettzimmer sind nach unterschiedlichen Themen gestaltet und bieten bis zu zehn Leuten Platz zum Übernachten. Eine Besonderheit ist die Hofbühne für Konzerte und andere Veranstaltungen.

Cette association éclectique d'hôtel design et d'auberge de jeunesse insuffle un vent nouveau dans le monde de l'hôtellerie. Ce concept, imaginé par l'architecte Aisslinger, est un patchwork décoratif innovant qui s'intègre dans la structure de lofts de cet ancien bâtiment industriel. Les 119 chambres simples et à plusieurs lits sont aménagées d'après différentes thématiques et peuvent loger jusqu'à dix personnes. Particularité : la scène de spectacles située dans la cour intérieure qui accueille divers concerts et événements.

Con su ecléctica mezcla de hotel de diseño y albergue juvenil, el Hotel Michelberger es un soplo de aire fresco en el sector. El diseño del berlinés studio aisslinger se integra innovadoramente en la estructura de loft de la antigua edificación industrial. Las 119 habitaciones individuales y múltiples han sido decoradas con temas muy diversos y pueden albergar hasta a diez personas. Cabe destacar el escenario del patio, donde se celebran conciertos y otros actos.

HOTEL MICHELBERGER

Warschauer Straße 39 // Friedrichshain
Tel.: +49 (0)30 29 77 85 90
www.michelbergerhotel.com

U1, S3, S5, S7, S75 Warschauer Straße

WERNER AISS

In his work as a product designer, Werner Aisslinger is primarily interested in the use of state-of-the-art technologies and unusual materials. He developed the world's first line of gel furniture, thus achieving a quantum leap in material evolution. As a result of his monumental success and accessible designs, Aisslinger has become the leading figure for a new generation, winning numerous design awards and guest lecturing at prestigious universities. His Juli Chair was the first German chair in 30 years to be selected for the permanent collection at the MoMA in New York. His Loftcube project involving mobile housing units reinterprets the living experience of today's urban dwellers: in the form of transportable homes, he offers urban nomads maximum freedom in a minimum of space. His latest coup is the design of the Hotel Michelberger, with which he has created an entirely new kind of hotel targeting young travelers who want a metropolitan experience not only on their forays into the city but also in their lodgings.

Werner Aisslinger interessiert sich bei seiner Arbeit als Produktdesigner vor allem für den Einsatz neuester Technologien und ungewöhnlicher Materialien. Er entwickelte eine weltweit neuartige Serie von Gelmöbeln und schaffte somit einen Quantensprung in der Materialevolution. Dank seines großen Erfolgs und seines eingängigen Designs wurde Aisslinger zur Leitfigur einer neuen Generation, gewann zahlreiche Designpreise und wurde als Gastdozent an renommierte Universitäten gerufen. Sein Juli Chair war der erste deutsche Stuhl seit 30 Jahren, der für die permanente Kollektion des MoMA in New York ausgewählt wurde. Sein Projekt Loftcube, eine mobile Wohneinheit, interpretiert das Lebensgefühl heutiger Großstadtmenschen neu: Als transportables Zuhause bietet er urbanen Nomaden größtmögliche Freiheit auf kleinstem Raum. Sein jüngster Coup ist das Design Hotel Michelberger – mit diesem Hotel schuf er einen völlig neuen Hoteltypus. Die Zielgruppe sind junge Reisende, die die Atmosphäre der Hauptstadt nicht nur auf Streifzügen durch die Stadt, sondern auch in ihrer Unterkunft erleben wollen.

SLINGER

Ce qui intéresse le plus Werner Aisslinger dans son travail de designer produit, c'est l'utilisation des nouvelles technologies et des matériaux insolites. Il développa une nouvelle gamme de meubles en gel et réalisa ainsi un progrès énorme dans l'évolution des matériaux. Grâce à son succès et son design des plus original, Aisslinger devint une icône de sa génération, remporta plusieurs prix et fut invité comme orateur dans les universités les plus réputées. Son modèle Juli Chair fut la première chaise allemande depuis 30 ans à faire partie de la collection permanente du MoMA de New York. Son projet Loftcube, un loft mobile, reflète la nouvelle génération des grandes villes : grâce à sa mobilité, ce bungalow permet aux nomades urbains de s'installer où bon leur semble en utilisant un espace moindre. Son dernier coup fut la transformation de l'Hotel Michelberger en un tout nouveau style d'hôtel bien particulier. Il cible surtout un public de jeunes voyageurs voulant s'imprégner de l'atmosphère de la capitale, qui se reflète non seulement dans ses promenades, mais aussi dans ses hébergements.

Desde su condición de diseñador de producción, Werner Aisslinger se interesa principalmente por la aplicación de nuevas tecnologías y materiales poco habituales. Ha diseñado una novedosísima serie de muebles en gel con la que ha dado un paso de gigante en la evolución de materiales. Gracias a su enorme éxito y a sus inconfundibles diseños, Aisslinger se ha convertido en faro de una nueva generación, al tiempo que ha obtenido numerosos premios de diseño y ha ejercido la docencia en universidades de reconocido prestigio. Su Juli Chair fue la primera silla alemana en 30 años en ser seleccionada para la colección permanente del MoMA neoyorquino. Su proyecto Loftcube, un módulo vivienda móvil, reinterpreta por completo la sensación vital del urbanita actual: su condición de hogar transportable ofrece a los nómadas urbanos una enorme libertad en un espacio muy reducido. Su más reciente golpe de efecto lo ha conseguido con el diseño del Hotel Michelberger, establecimiento para el que ha creado un nuevo concepto de hostelería. Busca su público entre viajeros jóvenes que desean empaparse de la atmósfera de la capital no sólo en sus paseos por la ciudad sino también en su alojamiento.

THEMROC

Torstraße 183 // Mitte
Tel.: +49 (0)162 4 25 11 21

Tue–Thu 5 pm to midnight,
Fri–Sat 7 pm to 2 am, Sun 7 pm to 11 pm
U8 Rosenthaler Platz

"You'll eat whatever is put on the table!" Oli and Ali, the co-owners as well as chefs, have transformed this maternal command into a gastronomical concept. The menu changes daily and food is served in a deliberately simple bistro style, without tablecloths or any other frills. An evening at Themroc feels more like a meal with friends than dinner at a restaurant. Though otherwise unconventional, Themroc is closed on Mondays.

„Es wird gegessen, was auf den Tisch kommt!" Oli und Ali, die beiden Besitzer und zugleich auch die Köche, haben die mütterliche Redensart zu einem Gastronomiekonzept verarbeitet. Serviert wird das täglich wechselnde Menü in bewusst einfacher Bistromanier, ganz ohne Tischtuch und sonstigem Schnickschnack. Ein Abend im Themroc gleicht eher einem Essen mit Freunden als einem Restaurantbesuch. Trotz allem Unkonventionellen ist Montag Ruhetag.

« On mange ce qui est servi à table ! », c'est la devise de cet établissement gastronomique qui rappelle la cuisine et l'ambiance de « chez maman », créé par Oli et Ali, les deux propriétaires et chefs cuisiniers. Une atmosphère de bistro où le menu varie chaque jour et est servi sans nappe et sans chichis. Une soirée au Themroc ressemble plus à un repas entre amis qu'à une visite au restaurant. Malgré son côté peu conventionnel, le restaurant est fermé le lundi.

"¿Qué hay para comer? Lo que hay en el plato". Oli y Ali, propietarios y al mismo tiempo cocineros, han adaptado el tradicional grito de guerra materno y lo han convertido en lema gastronómico. El menú diario, siempre diferente, se sirve al estilo de los bares, sin manteles ni demás fruslerías. Una velada en el Themroc no es tanto una visita al restaurante como una comida entre amigos. En un punto sí son convencionales: los lunes cierran por descanso del personal.

Their gastronomical offering isn't the only proof of the impeccable taste of the owners, interior designer Oliver Mahne and manager Hans Thedieck. The small corner café in the trendy district surrounding the Hackescher Markt is most notable for its furnishings, which combine natural wood floors with solid wooden tables and modern Eames chairs. Every few weeks changing artworks adorn the gray concrete wall.

Die beiden Besitzer, Interiordesigner Oliver Mahne und Geschäftsführer Hans Thedieck, beweisen nicht nur beim gastronomischen Angebot einen ausgewählten Geschmack. Das kleine Eckcafé im Trendviertel um den Hackeschen Markt fällt vor allem durch seine Einrichtung auf. Ein naturbelassener Dielenboden wird mit Massivholztischen und modernen Eames-Stühlen kombiniert. Die graue Betonwand ziert alle paar Wochen wechselnde Kunst.

Les deux propriétaires, décorateur d'intérieur Oliver Mahne, et gérant d'affaires Hans Thedieck, le gérant, ont su démontrer leur amour du goût en proposant des mets savoureux et en optant pour un aménagement séduisant. Ce petit café, situé dans un quartier branché au coin du Hackescher Markt, attire le regard des passants par l'originalité de son décor intérieur, où s'accorde le plancher naturel aux tables en bois massif et aux chaises design Eames. Toutes les deux ou trois semaines, le mur gris de béton est orné d'œuvres d'art différentes.

Los dos propietarios, el diseñador de interiores Oliver Mahne y el gerente Hans Thedieck, el gerente, un magnífico gusto, y no sólo en la oferta gastronómica. El pequeño café, ubicado en el muy apreciado barrio de Hackescher Markt, destaca principalmente por el diseño de su interior. Allí se ha combinado un suelo de madera sin tratar con macizas mesas de madera y modernas sillas Eames. La pared de hormigón gris se adorna cada pocas semanas con diferentes obras de arte.

OLIV

Münzstraße 8 // Mitte
Tel.: +49 (0)30 89 20 65 40
www.oliv-cafe.de

Mon–Fri 8.30 am to 7 pm, Sat 9.30 am to 7 pm,
Sun 10 am to 6 pm
U8 Weinmeisterstraße

D

Tucked away on the second floor of the Palais am Festungsgraben, an exotic world awaits visitors. Originally built for the Soviet pavilion at the 1974 Leipzig Trade Fair to represent Tajikistan culture, the tea room remained in the possession of the Society for German-Soviet Friendship. In a room decorated with Persian carpets, guests are seated on traditional Ikat cushions at knee-high tables and enjoy tea, pastries and Russian or international specialties.

Versteckt in der ersten Etage des Palais am Festungsgraben eröffnet sich dem Besucher eine exotische Welt. Auf der Leipziger Messe 1974 zur Repräsentation tadschikischer Kultur im sowjetischen Pavillon errichtet, verblieb die Teestube danach im Besitz der Gesellschaft für deutsch-sowjetische Freundschaft. In einem mit tadshikischen Teppichen geschmückten Raum sitzt der Gast auf Kissen mit traditionellen Ikat-Mustern an kniehohen Tischen und genießt Tee, Gebäck und russische oder internationale Spezialitäten.

À l'étage d'un vieux palais du Festungsgraben, le visiteur sera transporté dans un monde exotique. Ce salon de thé, créé à l'occasion de la foire de Leipzig en 1974 en vue de représenter la culture tadjik dans le pavillon soviétique, est resté depuis la propriété de la Société pour l'amitié germano-soviétique. Le visiteur pourra se détendre sur des coussins aux motifs Ikat et savourer du thé, des pâtisseries, des spécialités russes et internationales à une table basse dans un décor composé de tapis persans.

Oculto en la primera planta del Palais de Festungsgraben, un mundo exótico espera al visitante atento. Creado en representación de la cultura tadjika en el pabellón soviético de la Feria de Leipzig de 1974, el local quedó más tarde en posesión de la Sociedad para la Promoción de la Amistad Germano-Soviética. Rodeado de alfombras persas, el comensal se sienta en cojines de tradicional dibujo ikat frente a mesillas a medida y puede disfrutar del té, las pastas y las especialidades rusas e internacionales de la casa.

TADSHIKISCHE TEESTUBE

Am Festungsgraben 1 // Mitte
Tel.: +49 (0)30 2 04 11 12

Mon–Fri 5 pm to midnight, Sat+Sun 3 pm to midnight
U6, S1, S2, S3, S7, S25, S75 Friedrichstraße

In times of fast food and slow food, Asian cuisine has proved to be a healthy middle way that doesn't take much time. In a bustling atmosphere, Thai street food specialties are prepared in the open kitchen using primarily organic products, and served at long ash tables. Simple benches foster communicative closeness to the next party while tall lamps spread muted light.

In Zeiten von Fast- und Slowfood hat sich die asiatische Küche als gesunder und schnell zu genießender Mittelweg erwiesen. In einer geschäftigen Atmosphäre werden Spezialitäten der thailändischen Street Kitchen aus vorwiegend biologisch erzeugten Produkten in der offenen Küche zubereitet und an langen Eschenholztischen serviert. Einfache Bänke als Sitzmöbel sorgen für eine kommunikative Nähe zum Tischnachbarn, während große Lampen gedämpftes Licht verbreiten.

A l'ère du fast et du slow food, la cuisine asiatique s'avère être le meilleur compromis pour une alimentation saine et rapide. Des spécialités de la cuisine de rue thaïlandaise à base de produits essentiellement biologiques sont préparées dans une cuisine ouverte et servis sur des longues tables en frêne dans une atmosphère dynamique. Un aménagement simple, composé de bancs, et de lampes diffusant une lumière tamisée, crée une ambiance intime qui favorise le contact avec son voisin de table.

Ante la disyuntiva fast-food–slow food, la cocina asiática se ha revelado como un punto medio sano y rápido. En este local de ajetreado ambiente se sirven especialidades de la cocina callejera tailandesa: los ingredientes, mayoritariamente procedentes de cultivos biológicos, se preparan en una cocina abierta y se sirven en largas mesas de fresno. Los sencillos bancos facilitan y promueven la comunicación con los vecinos de mesa a la tenue luz que proporcionan las enormes lámparas del local.

CHA CHÀ POSITIVE EATING

Friedrichstraße 63 // Mitte
Tel.: +49 (0)30 20 62 59 60
www.eatchacha.com

Mon–Fri noon to 10 pm, Sat 6 pm to 10 pm
U2, U6 Stadtmitte

Based on her many years of experience as a culture and lifestyle journalist and editor, Hamburg-native Birgit von Heintze established her interior design studio in 1997 where she develops individual furnishing concepts for living and work spaces. She recently opened a small, elegant showroom where she presents lovingly chosen furniture, lamps, fabrics, and home accessories.

Mit ihrer längjährigen Erfahrung als Journalistin und Redakteurin für Kultur und Lebensstil gründete die aus Hamburg stammende Birgit von Heintze 1997 ihr Unternehmen für Interior Design, mit dem sie individuelle Einrichtungskonzepte für Lebens- und Arbeitsräume entwickelt. Neu eröffnet hat sie ihren kleinen, feinen Showroom in dem sie liebevoll ausgewählte Möbel, Lampen, Stoffe und Wohnaccessoires präsentiert.

Birgit von Heintze, originaire de Hambourg, met à profit son expérience de journaliste et rédactrice de rubriques sur la culture et l'art de vivre pour fonder en 1997 son entreprise de décoration d'intérieur, où elle crée des aménagements décoratifs pour habitations privées ou bureaux. Dans son élégant petit showroom, qui a récemment ouvert ses portes, sont présentés des meubles, des lampes, des tissus et des accessoires mobiliers sélectionnés par ses propres soins.

Sobre la base de su larga experiencia como periodista y redactora de cultura y lifestyle, Birgit von Heintze fundó en 1997 su empresa de interiorismo, a través de la cual desarrolla modelos individuales de decoración para viviendas y espacios de trabajo. Recientemente ha inaugurado un discreto y elegante showroom en el que presenta primorosos y selectos muebles, lámparas, telas y accesorios del hogar.

BIRGIT VON HEINTZE INTERIORS

Sredzkistraße 52 // Prenzlauer Berg
Tel.: +49 (0)30 75 56 93 49
www.birgit-von-heintze.de

Tue–Fri 12 am to 7 pm, Sat 11 am to 4 pm
U2 Eberswalderstraße

LUNETTES SELECTION

Torstraße 172 // Mitte
Tel.: +49 (0)30 20 21 52 16
www.lunettes-selection.de

Mon–Fri noon to 8 pm, Sat noon to 6 pm
U8 Rosenthaler Platz

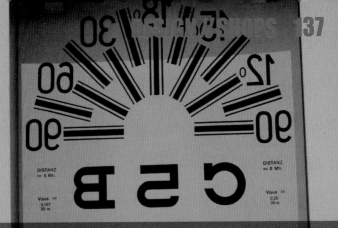

Lunettes Selection has long been a mecca for vintage eyewear fans. These specialists in unusual frames recently opened a second boutique on Torstraße, which is well on its way to becoming the shopping mile of central Berlin. In addition to a cross-section of 20th-century eyeglass designs, shoppers can now purchase eyewear from the collection of the head of Lunettes, Uta Geyer, which she designs exclusively for her stores.

Für Liebhaber von Vintagebrillen ist die Lunettes Brillenagentur schon seit längerem ein Begriff. Auf der Torstraße, die immer mehr zur Shoppingmeile in Berlins neuer Mitte avanciert, eröffneten die Spezialisten für ausgefallene Gestelle kürzlich eine zweite Boutique. Neben einem Querschnitt an seit 1900 entworfenen Brillenmodellen kann erstmals auch die Kollektion von Chefin Uta Geyer erworben werden, die sie exklusiv für ihren Laden entworfen hat.

La boutique est la référence pour tous les amoureux de lunettes vintage. Les spécialistes des montures insolites ont ouvert une seconde boutique sur la Torstraße, l'avenue commerçante la plus en vue du nouveau centre de Berlin. Hormis les modèles de lunettes créés depuis 1900, le visiteur pourra admirer la collection de la propriétaire des lieux, Uta Geyer, exclusivement créée pour sa boutique.

La agencia de optometristas Lunette es de sobras conocida por los amantes de las gafas retro. Recientemente, los especialistas en monturas poco habituales han abierto un segundo local en la Torstraße, que poco a poco se ha convertido en la avenida comercial del nuevo centro de Berlín. Además de un muestrario de modelos que abarca incluso los fabricados hacia 1900, la tienda ofrece también la colección de la propietaria Uta Geyer, diseñada en exclusiva para el local.

D

Inspired by the dandies of yesteryear, this Berlin atelier releases two collections per year aimed at fashion-conscious men. Garments are made to measure for the customer from the finest Italian cloth, and furnished with individual details. Customers can even create their own personal look in collaboration with designer Itamar Zechoval. The right accessories—such as a hat by an Italian manufacturer or a handmade walking stick—complete the outfit.

Inspiriert durch die Dandies vergangener Zeiten präsentiert das Berliner Atelier jährlich zwei Kollektionen für modebewusste Herren. Aus feinsten italienischen Stoffen werden maßgeschneiderte Modelle für den Kunden angefertigt und mit individuellen Details versehen. Zusammen mit dem Designer Itamar Zechoval kann der Kunde seinen persönlichen Look kreieren. Mit dem richtigen Accessoire, wie dem Hut einer italienischen Manufaktur oder einem handgefertigten Gehstock, wird das Outfit abgerundet.

S'inspirant du style de dandy du siècle passé, l'atelier berlinois présente deux collections annuelles pour les amateurs de mode masculine. Des modèles à base de précieuses étoffes italiennes et aux détails individuels sont confectionnés sur mesure pour le client. Avec l'aide du designer Itamar Zechoval, le client peut même créer son propre look. L'accessoire adéquat, un chapeau de confection italienne et une canne faite main, complètent la tenue vestimentaire.

Los dandys de antaño son la inspiración para este taller berlinés, que cada año presenta dos elegantísimas colecciones para hombre. A partir de las mejores telas italianas se confeccionan en él trajes a medida para los clientes, que se adornan luego con detalles individualizados. En colaboración con el diseñador Itamar Zechoval el cliente puede incluso crear su propio look. Un complemento adecuado, como un sombrero de factura italiana o un bastón tallado a mano, servirá para redondear el atuendo.

DANDY OF THE GROTESQUE

Gormannstraße 17 b // Mitte
Tel.: +49 (0)30 24 04 82 80
www.dandyofthegrotesque.com

Tue–Sat 11 am to 6 pm and by appointment
U8 Rosenthaler Platz

D

Since becoming hat designer to such stars as Christina Aguilera and Brad Pitt, Fiona Bennett has achieved fame on an international scale. She produces her unusual headgear at her salon near the Hackescher Markt in Berlin's Mitte district. Each hat is a unique, handmade creation and can, on request, be personally fitted to the customer's head by Ms. Bennett herself. The salon and shop can be visited by appointment only.

Seit die Hutdesignerin Stars wie Christina Aguilera und Brad Pitt zu ihren Kunden zählt, ist Fiona Bennett auch international bekannt. Die ausgefallenen Modelle stellt sie in ihrem Atelier unweit des Hackeschen Marktes in Berlin-Mitte her. Jeder Hut ist ein handgefertigtes Unikat und wird bei Bedarf von Frau Bennett auch persönlich dem Kopf des Kunden angepasst. Das Atelier und Geschäft ist nur nach Vereinbarung geöffnet.

Depuis que des vedettes telles que Christina Aguilera et Brad Pitt comptent parmi les clients de la chapelière, Fiona Bennett est devenue mondialement connue. Elle crée ses modèles les plus insolites dans son atelier près du Hackescher Markt dans le centre de Berlin. Chaque modèle, entièrement fait à la main, est une pièce unique et aux mesures de la tête du client. L'atelier-boutique n'accueille ses clients que sur rendez-vous.

Desde que la diseñadora de sombreros cuenta entre sus clientes a estrellas como Christina Aguilera y Brad Pitt, el nombre de Fiona Bennett suena con fuerza en todo el mundo. Confecciona sus llamativos modelos en un taller propio, no muy lejos de Hackescher Markt. Cada pieza es única, realizada enteramente a mano, y la propia diseñadora se encarga de ajustarlo a la cabeza del cliente cuando es necesario. El acceso a la tienda y el taller sólo es posible mediante cita previa.

SALON BENNETT

Alte Schönhauser Straße 35 // Mitte
Tel.: +49 (0)30 28 09 63 30
www.fionabennett.com

By appointment
U8 Weinmeisterstraße

SCHÖNHAUSER DESIGN

Neue Schönhauser Straße 18 // Mitte
Tel.: +49 (0)30 2 81 17 04
www.schoenhauser-design.de

Mon–Sat noon to 8 pm
U8 Weinmeisterstraße

As a well-known institution offering home accessories and unique souvenirs, this store on the Neue Schönhauser Straße shopping mile is here to stay. Since 1997, lovers of retro and all manner of East German nostalgia have been able to buy new and used designer classics as well as household objects—and can now even lease them.

Als bekannte Institution für Wohnaccessoires und ausgefallene Souvenirs ist der Laden von der Shoppingmeile der Neuen Schönhauser Straße nicht mehr wegzudenken. Seit 1997 können Liebhaber von Retrodesign und „ostalgischem" Allerlei aus DDR-Zeiten hier gebrauchte und neue Designklassiker sowie Wohnobjekte kaufen und neuerdings bei Bedarf sogar mieten.

Cette institution, réputée pour ses accessoires mobiliers et ses articles souvenirs insolites, reste un lieu incontournable à visiter sur la rue commerçante de la Neue Schönhauser Straße. Depuis 1997, les amoureux du design rétro et les « estalgiques » de la RDA y trouvent leur bonheur en y achetant ou louant des classiques du design et du mobilier (neuf ou de location).

El establecimiento sito en la zona comercial de Neue Schönhauser Straße es toda una institución como proveedor de complementos para el hogar. Desde 1997, los partidarios del diseño retro y los nostálgicos de la RDA pueden comprar aquí (y desde hace poco incluso alquilar) clásicos del diseño, nuevos y de segunda mano, y también propiedades inmobiliarias.

BUCHHANDLUNG WALTHER KÖNIG

Burgstraße 27 // Mitte
Tel.: +49 (0)30 25 76 09 80
www.buchhandlung-walther-koenig.de

Mon–Sat 10 am to 8 pm
S3, S5, S7, S75 Hackescher Markt

In a generous 3.800-sq.-ft. space lavishly stocked with books on art, architecture, photography, design, and much more, the Berlin branch of the famous Cologne-based bookstore is second to none. Experience gained over many years has made this bookstore the go-to place when it comes to art books. The shop itself is always worth a visit, with its views of the Berlin Cathedral and Museum Island.

Mit einer großzügigen Fläche von 350 m², prall gefüllt mit Büchern zu Kunst, Architektur, Fotografie, Design und vielem mehr, steht die Berliner Filiale dem berühmten Kölner Stammhaus in nichts nach. Über Jahre erworbene Erfahrungen machen die Buchhandlung zu einer der Topadressen, wenn es um Kunstbücher geht. Ein Besuch im Geschäft mit Blick auf Berliner Dom und Museuminsel lohnt sich immer.

Avec ses 350 m² de surface et sa multitude de livres sur l'art, l'architecture, la photographie, le design et plus encore, la filiale berlinoise n'a rien à envier à sa maison mère de Cologne. Grâce à ses années d'expérience, cette librairie est devenue le lieu incontournable pour les amoureux des livres d'art. Un détour par cet antre de la littérature artistique avec vue sur le dôme de Berlin et l'île des musées vaut toujours la peine.

Con sus extensos 350 m² llenos a rebosar de libros de arte, arquitectura, fotografía, diseño y mucho más, la filial berlinesa de la conocida librería de Colonia no tiene nada que envidiar a la sede principal. La experiencia acumulada a lo largo de los años hacen del establecimiento una dirección indispensable en lo tocante a volúmenes de arte. Vale siempre la pena acercarse a echar un vistazo al local, con vistas a la catedral de Berlín y la Isla de los Museos.

QUARTIER 206

Friedrichstraße 71 // Mitte
Tel.: +49 (0)30 20 94 65 00
www.quartier206.com

Mon–Fri 10.30 am to 7.30 pm, Sat 10 am to 6 pm
U6 Französische Straße, U2, U6 Stadtmitte

With Quartier 206, planned in 1997 as a retail, residential and office building, initiators Anno August and Anne Maria Jagdfeld sought to revive the golden age of Friedrichstraße. The interior of the complex, planned by architects Pei, Cobb, Freed & Partners and oriented to the Art Deco style, radiates Mediterranean grandeur with its atrium dominated by mosaic floors and curving stairs. A star-shaped skylight illuminates the shopping arcade with its exclusive boutiques like Gucci, Louis Vuitton, and Bottega Veneta.

Mit ihrem 1997 als Wohn- und Geschäftshaus geplanten Quartier 206 wollten die Initiatoren Anno August und Anne Maria Jagdfeld die goldenen Zeiten der Friedrichstraße wieder aufleben lassen. Das Interieur des von den Architekten Pei, Cobb, Freed & Partners geplanten, am Stil des Art déco orientierten Gebäudekomplexes strahlt mit seinem von Mosaikböden und geschwungenen Treppen dominierten Atrium mediterrane Grandezza aus. Ein sternförmiges Oberlicht erhellt die Einkaufspassage mit ihren Edelboutiquen von Gucci, Louis Vuitton oder Bottega Veneta.

Réalisé en 1997 par les architectes Anno August et Anne Maria Jagdfeld, ce complexe d'habitations et de magasins fait revivre l'âge d'or de la Friedrichstraße. L'architecture intérieure, imaginée par Pei, Cobb, Freed & Partners, reflète le style art déco de l'édifice avec son atrium mediterrane aux sols de mosaïques et aux escaliers hélicoïdaux. Un lanterneau en forme d'étoile éclaire la galerie marchande avec ses boutiques de luxe comme Gucci, Louis Vuitton ou Bottega Veneta.

Anno August y Anne Maria Jagdfeld, promotores del espacio comercial, de viviendas y negocios Quartier 206, pretendieron reactivar la época dorada de la Friedrichstraße. El interior del complejo arquitectónico, diseñado por Pei, Cobb, Freed & Partners y de clara inspiración art déco, irradia grandiosidad mediterránea con sus suelos de mosaico y un atrio dominado por curvilíneas escaleras. El lucernario en forma de estrella ilumina la galería comercial, que alberga establecimientos de lujo como Gucci, Louis Vuitton o Bottega Veneta.

Established in 1998, this large Berlin furniture store moved to its present location in 2008. Behind a 19th-century industrial building facade, the 65,000-sq.-ft. store located directly on the river Spree offers six floors of furniture, lamps and décor for home and office, with everything from classics to unusual designer pieces. A unique feature of Exil: the size of all tables can be customized to meet the client's needs.

1998 gegründet, bezog das große Berliner Einrichtungshaus 2008 neue Räume. Hinter der Fassade eines Industriegebäudes aus der Gründerzeit bietet das direkt an der Spree gelegene Haus auf 6 000 m², verteilt über sechs Etagen, Möbel, Lampen und Dekoration für die Privatwohnung und das Büro. Das Angebot reicht von Klassikern bis hin zu ausgefallenen Designstücken. Eine Besonderheit: Alle Tische können je nach Kundenwunsch in ihrer Größe angepasst werden.

Fondé en 1998, ce magasin de meubles berlinois a rouvert ses portes au sein de nouveaux locaux en 2008. Ce bâtiment industriel du XIXe siècle, situé le long de la Spree, propose sur une surface de 6 000 m² répartie sur six étages des meubles, des lampes, des articles de décoration pour bureaux et habitations privées. La gamme de produits varie des modèles classiques aux pièces design les plus insolites. Particularité : les tables peuvent être faites sur mesure à la demande du client.

Fundada en 1998, la gran tienda berlinesa de interiorismo se trasladó en 2008 a un nuevo local. Tras la fachada de una antigua nave industrial del siglo XIX construida junto al Spree, la tienda ofrece sobre sus 6 000 m² (repartidos en seis plantas) muebles, lámparas y decoración para hogar y oficina. Aquí pueden encontrarse tanto muebles clásicos como sorprendentes piezas de diseño. Una curiosidad: si el cliente así lo desea, es posible adaptar el tamaño de todas las mesas.

EXIL WOHNMAGAZIN

Köpenicker Straße 18–20 // Kreuzberg
Tel.: +49 (0)30 21 73 61 90
www.exil-wohnmagazin.de

Mon–Fri 11 am to 7 pm, Sat 11 am to 6 pm
U1 Schlesisches Tor

Beneath the railway tracks, lovers of art, design, photography, film, and architecture books will find all that their hearts desire—regardless of whether they're looking for a reference work or a rarity. The abundantly-stocked shelves of this specialized bookstore established in 1980 encourage extensive browsing. In addition to recent publications, there is also an antiquarian section organized by subjects. A selection of the stock can also be viewed and ordered online.

Unter vier Stadtbahnbögen finden Liebhaber von Büchern zu Kunst, Design, Fotografie, Film und Architektur alles, was das Herz begehrt – ganz gleich, ob sie ein Standardwerk oder eine Rarität suchen. Die prall gefüllten Regale der 1980 gegründeten Fachbuchhandlung laden zum ausgiebigen Stöbern ein, denn zusätzlich zu den aktuellen Neuerscheinungen gibt es ein nach Sachgebieten unterteiltes Antiquariat. Eine Auswahl des Sortiments kann auch online eingesehen und bestellt werden.

Située sous les quatre viaducs du réseau ferroviaire berlinois, cette librairie offre aux amoureux des livres d'art, de design, de photographie, de cinéma et d'architecture tout ce qu'ils désirent, que ce soit un ouvrage de référence ou une rareté. Les étagères aux mille trésors de cette librairie spécialisée datant de 1980 vous invitent à venir faire vos emplettes, que vous cherchiez une édition actuelle ou même une antiquité. Les différents ouvrages sont également disponibles en ligne.

Bajo cuatro arcos del tren elevado, los apasionados de los libros de arte, diseño, fotografía y cine encontrarán todo cuanto puedan desear, tanto obras básicas como auténticas rarezas. Los repletos estantes de esta librería especializada, fundada en 1980, invitan a curiosear durante horas, ya que además de los más recientes lanzamientos ofrece también una sección de anticuario ordenada temáticamente. Es posible también consultar y adquirir online una selección de su catálogo.

BÜCHERBOGEN SAVIGNYPLATZ

Stadtbahnbogen 593 // Charlottenburg
Tel.: +49 (0)30 3 18 69 50
www.buecherbogen.com

Mon–Fri 10 am to 8 pm, Sat 10 am to 7 pm
S3, S5, S7, S75 Savignyplatz

VILLA HARTENECK

Douglasstraße 9 // Grunewald
Tel.: +49 (0)30 89 72 78 90
www.villa-harteneck.de

Mon–Fri 10 am to 7 pm, Sat 10 am to 6 pm
S7 Grunewald

Built in 1911 as a private residence for the chemical manufacturer Carl Harteneck, the Neoclassical villa with its Italian-style gardens is now a show-room for luxurious interior furnishings. This modern store offers household accessories, flowers, garden furniture, books, and entire furnishing concepts aimed at customers with discriminating taste. It is also possible to rent individual rooms or the entire villa, including all services, for events.

1911 als Privatresidenz für den Chemie-fabrikanten Carl Harteneck erbaut, dient die neoklassizistische Villa mit ihrem nach italienischem Vorbild gestalteten Landschaftsgarten heute als Verkaufs-raum für luxuriöse Inneneinrichtungen. Das moderne Ladenkonzept bietet dem anspruchsvollen Kunden Wohnacces-soires, Floristik, Gartenmöbel, Bücher und ganze Einrichtungskonzepte. Für Veranstaltungen können sowohl einzel-ne Räume als auch die gesamte Villa in-klusive Rundumservice gemietet werden.

Cette villa de style néoclassique avec son jardin paysager de style italien, bâtie en 1911 pour le fabricant de produits chimiques, Carl Harteneck, est au-jourd'hui une salle de vente de mobilier de luxe. Ce magasin moderne propose au client une variété d'accessoires de décoration, d'articles de floristique, de meubles de jardin, de livres et d'amé-nagements décoratifs. Certaines salles ou la villa entière, avec service complet, peuvent être louées pour l'organisation d'événements.

Construida en 1911 como residencia privada del industrial químico Carl Har-teneck, la villa neoclasicista y sus jardi-nes de inspiración italiana sirven hoy como sala de exposición de interiorismo de lujo. En este moderno concepto de tienda, los más exigentes encontrarán complementos para el hogar, floriste-ría, libros y propuestas completas de interiorismo. Es posible alquilar tanto la villa completa como determinadas salas (con servicio incluido) para la organización de eventos.

KINO INTERNATIONAL

Karl-Marx-Allee 33 // Mitte
Tel.: +49 (0)30 24 75 60 11
www.yorck.de

U5 Schillingstraße

A visit to former East Germany's premier film theater is like a journey to an earlier age. Visitors find the atmosphere of this movie theater to be extremely appealing, in no small part because of the original and largely preserved '60s-era interior that radiates socialist charm. Absolutely unique to this theater are the large film posters that were hand painted for the "Inter."

Ein Kinobesuch im ehemaligen Premierenkino der DDR gleicht einer Reise in längst vergangene Zeiten. Seine Besucher schätzen die Atmosphäre des Lichtspielhauses nicht zuletzt wegen der größtenteils erhaltenen originalen Einrichtung aus den 60er Jahren, die den Charme des Sozialismus versprüht. Eine absolute Besonderheit sind die großformatigen Filmplakate, die für das „Inter" noch von Hand gemalt werden.

Aller voir un film dans l'ancien cinéma datant de l'époque de la RDA est un voyage dans le temps. Ce n'est pas seulement l'atmosphère de cette salle de projection qui séduit les visiteurs, mais bien l'aménagement intérieur qui rappelle les années 60, l'époque où la culture socialiste florissait. Coup de cœur de ce lieu insolite sont les affiches de film peintes à la main.

Una tarde de cine en el que fuera escenario de los estrenos cinematográficos de la RDA es como un viaje a un pasado remoto. Los espectadores saben apreciar el ambiente, y en especial la decoración original de la década de 1960, que irradia el encanto del socialismo. Particularmente llamativos resultan los enormes carteles publicitarios, pintados todavía a mano para el "Inter".

ART

ARCHITECTURE

Location	N°	page	page	N°	Location
Seven Star Gallery	**1**	10	60	**18**	Aedes am Pfefferberg
Me Collectors Room Berlin	**2**	12	62	**19**	Neues Museum
KW Institute of Contemporary Art	**3**	14	66	**20**	Jakob-und-Wilhelm-Grimm-Zentrum
C/O Berlin	**4**	16	68	**21**	Collegium Hungaricum Berlin
Sammlung Boros	**5**	18	70	**22**	Deutsches Historisches Museum
Contemporary Fine Arts	**6**	24	72	**23**	Niederländische Botschaft
Museum The Kennedys	**7**	26	74	**24**	Hochschule für Musik Hanns Eisler
Galerie Thomas Schulte	**8**	28	76	**25**	Mini Loft
Galerie Ulrich Fiedler	**9**	30	78	**26**	Band des Bundes
East Side Gallery	**10**	32	82	**27**	Akademie der Künste
Berlinische Galerie	**11**	36	84	**28**	Denkmal für die ermordeten
Martin-Gropius-Bau	**12**	40			Juden Europas
Neue Nationalgalerie	**13**	42	86	**29**	Science Center Medizintechnik
Hamburger Bahnhof –			90	**30**	E-Werk
Museum für Gegenwart Berlin	**14**	44	94	**31**	Topographie des Terrors
Helmut Newton Stiftung			96	**32**	Jüdisches Museum Berlin
im Museum für Fotografie	**15**	46	100	**33**	Liquidrom
Camera Work	**16**	50	102	**34**	Bauhaus-Archiv Berlin
Haus am Waldsee	**17**	52	104	**35**	Philologische Bibliothek

MAP 157

PRENZLAUER BERG

Before the fall of the Wall in 1989, when the district was still neglected, a small sub and counter culture settled in its crumbling old houses. Today almost all buildings are renovated, and young families with kids are mingling with artists and foreign adventurers in trendy cafés and boutiques.

MITTE

Here the city's past and present meet, creating a visually challenging blend. From the high-rise buildings that reminiscent of socialist times to charming cobbled streets, from ancient treasures to prestigious modern art, Mitte is a mecca for shoppers and hipsters from all over the world.

FRIEDRICHSHAIN/ KREUZBERG/NEUKÖLLN

With countless backyard galleries, bars, parks, and clubs these districts are hard to resist. Friedrichshain is popular with students and young families while still keeping a punk attitude. Kreuzberg houses a big Turkish community, artists and bon vivants. Between bohemian and bourgeois, the up-and-coming Neukölln has a unique appeal, also thanks to a strong Turkish-Arabic population.

DESIGN

page	N°	Location
112	**36**	Ackselhaus & Blue Home
114	**37**	Soho House Berlin
116	**38**	Hotel Amano
118	**39**	Cosmo Hotel Berlin
120	**40**	Hotel Michelberger
126	**41**	Themroc
128	**42**	Oliv
130	**43**	Tadshikische Teestube
132	**44**	Cha Chà Positive Eating
134	**45**	Birgit von Heintze Interiors
136	**46**	Lunettes Selection
138	**47**	Dandy of the Grotesque
140	**48**	Salon Bennett
142	**49**	Schönhauser Design
144	**50**	Buchhandlung Walther König
146	**51**	Quartier 206
148	**52**	Exil Wohnmagazin
150	**53**	Bücherbogen Savignyplatz
152	**54**	Villa Harteneck
154	**55**	Kino International

SCHÖNEBERG/ CHARLOTTENBURG/ TIERGARTEN

Like a well-off lady who knew wild times but has aged in dignity these districts are charming without the pressure to be hip. Schöneberg is a friendly, colorful place with a large gay community. In the more bourgeois Charlottenburg traces of the Golden Twenties still linger, there is excellent art, shopping and eating facilities. Tiergarten is named after its huge oasis, the Tiergarten park.

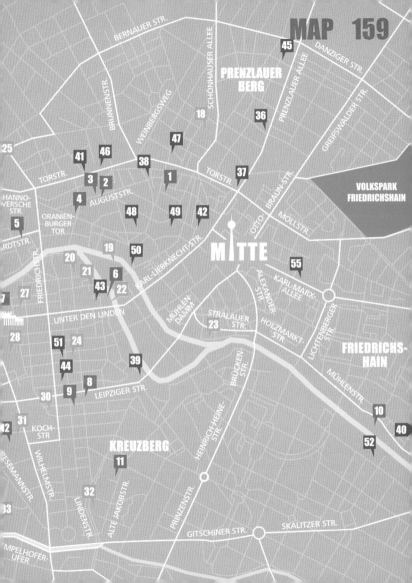

EMERGENCY

Ambulance/Fire Tel.: 112
Police   Tel.: 110

ARRIVAL

BY PLANE

Information on airports and security
regulations: Tel.: +49 (0)1 80 5 00 01 86
www.berlin-airport.de

SCHÖNEFELD AIRPORT (SFX)

18 km / 11 miles south of the city center. National and international flights. Free
shuttle service or 5–10 min. walk from
terminal to train station. For city center,
take S9, Regionalbahn or Airport Express
to Friedrichstraße or Zoologischer Garten
(30–45 min.).

TEGEL AIRPORT (TXL)

8 km / 5 miles north-west of the city center. National and international flights.
Take bus no. 128 from terminal to Kurt-
Schumacher-Platz subway station. Take U6
to Friedrichstraße (30 min.), bus no. 109/
express bus X9 to Zoologischer Garten (via
U7 Jakob-Kaiser-Platz, 20–30 min.) or TXL
Express Bus to Alexanderplatz (via Hauptbahnhof and Friedrichstraße, 35 min.).

BY TRAIN: BERLINER HAUPTBAHNHOF

Europaplatz 1
www.hbf-berlin.de – Berlin's magnificent
new Central Train Station is located close
to the new city center and the Reichstag.
Direct connection to local lines S3, S5, S7,
S75. Tel.: +49 (0)800 1 50 70 90 (auto-
matic timetable information), +49 (0)118
61 (travel service).
www.bahn.de – Official website of the
Deutsche Bahn

TOURIST INFORMATION

Berlin Tourismus Marketing (BTM)
Am Karlsbad 11
10785 Berlin
Tel.: +49 (0)30 25 00 25
Fax: +49 (0)30 25 00 24 24

information@btm.de (to order information material), reservierung@btm.de
(ticket and hotel reservations, vacation
packages), phone service Mon–Fri 8 am to
7 pm and Sat–Sun 9 am to 6 pm.
Berlin info stores are located at: Hauptbahnhof, Level 0, northern entrance,
Brandenburg Gate, Alexanderplatz, Neues
Kranzler Eck, Kurfürstendamm 21, Berlin
Pavillon am Reichstag, Scheidemannstr.
and Europa Center, Budapester Str. 45.
Further information points can be found at
the airports.

www.berlin.de – Official website of Berlin
www.btm.de – Berlin tourism marketing website
www.visitberlin.de – Comprehensive on-line tourist guide
www.berliner-stadtplan.com – City maps

ACCOMMODATION

www.berlin-tourist-information.de – Hotel booking service of Berlin Tourismus Marketing
www.berlinzimmer.de – Hotels, bed & breakfast, rooms, etc.
www.berliner-hotelzimmer.de – Hotels and bed & breakfast

TICKETS

www.hekticket.de – Wide range of tickets for concerts, cabaret, theater and other events in Berlin

Berlin WelcomeCard – Free trips on all public transportation in the specified, VBB region (fare regions A, B, and C) as well as a 50% discount on tickets for over 120 different tourist attractions and cultural venues for adults and up to three children under 15. Available online at cash machines as well as in the Berlin infostores, numerous hotels, BVG and S-Bahn ticket machines, etc. A ticket for 48 hours costs 16 €, ticket for 72 hours costs 22 €

GETTING AROUND

PUBLIC TRANSPORTATION

www.bvg.de – Berliner Verkehrsbetriebe – BVG, Tel.: +49 (0)30 1 94 49
www.s-bahn-berlin.de – S-Bahn Berlin, Tel.: +49 (0)30 29 74 33 33

TAXI

Tel.: +49 (0)30 26 10 26
Tel.: +49 (0)30 44 33 22
Tel.: +49 (0)8 00 2 22 22 55
Tel.: +49 (0)8 00 2 63 00 00

BICYCLE RENTALS

http://fahrradstation.de – Tel.: +49 (0)1 80 5 10 80 00. Rent: 10 €/day
www.callabike-interaktiv.de – Registration Tel.: +49 (0)7 00 (0)5 22 55 22 (from 6.2 ct/min.) or register online. Rent is 7 ct/min. or max. enter 15 €/day (24 hrs); bicycles are rented via cell phone, payment is by credit card or direct debit
http://bbbike.radzeit.de/cgi-bin/bbbike.cgi – Bicycle route finder for Berlin (BBBike)

CAR RENTAL

Beside the international rental car companies there are some Berlin based like:

www.robben-wientjes.de
www.allround.de
www.esautovermietung.de
www.lex.de
www.autos-weine.de

CITY TOURS

BUSES AND TRAMWAYS

Taking the bus or tram is the cheapest way of touring the city. Bus no. 100 and bus no. 200, which run between Bahnhof Zoo and Alexanderplatz, pass some of the main attractions. A tramway ride on line M1 takes you from Bahnhof Friedrichstraße to Prenzlauer Berg, passing the famous Hackesche Höfe and the Scheunenviertel on the way.

SIGHTSEEING BUSES

www.berolina-berlin.com – Berolina Sightseeing, Tel.: +49 (0)30 88 56 80 30
www.bbsberlin.de – Berliner-Bären-Stadtrundfahrt, Tel.: +49 (0)30 35 19 52 70
www.severin-kuehn-berlin.de – Severin & Kühn, Tel.: +49 (0)30 8 80 41 90

BOAT TOURS

www.sternundkreis.de – Stern- und Kreis-schifffahrt, Tel.: +49 (0)30 53 63 60-0
www.reedereiwinkler.de – Reederei Winkler, Tel.: +49 (0)30 34 99 59 33

GUIDED TOURS

www.artberlin-online.de – Art:berlin, Tel.: +49 (0)30 28 09 63 90 – In organized themed tours you get to know Berlin's cultural, artistic and urban landscapes.
http://stattreisenberlin.de/berlin – StattReisen Berlin, Tel.: +49 (0)30 4 55 30 28 – Walks around the city with a focus on history, society and politics.
www.stadtverfuehrung.de – Stadtverführung, Malmöer Str. 6, Tel.: +49 (0)30 4 44 09 36 – Tours on historical or contemporary themes.

ART & ARCHITECTURAL TOURS

www.visitberlin.de/english/sightseeing/e_si_architektur.php – This link contains several options for architectural tours
www.nicheberlin.de – Special insider tours beyond the known icons
www.berlin-info.com/e_prg_touren.html – Offers about ten different tours on architecture in Berlin
www.architecture-in-berlin.com – Individual tours in the so called "open air museum for architecture"
www.ticket-b.de – Guided sightseeing tours with architects

ART & CULTURE

www.art-in-berlin.de – Current and permanent exhibitions and museums
www.smb.spk-berlin.de – Official website of the National Museums in Berlin
www.stadtentwicklung.berlin.de/denkmal – Information on the most significant monuments in Berlin
www.museumsportal-berlin.de – Features and information about 200 museums, castles, historical and cultural sites and monuments.
www.indexberlin.de – Art event calendar
www.berliner-galerien.de – Galleries Association of Berlin (LVBG) is the professional representation of art galleries in Berlin
www.galerien-berlin-mitte.de – Calendar of art shows in galleries of Berlin Mitte
www.kulturprojekte-berlin.de – KulturProjekte Berlin is a not-for-profit organisation that works for the promotion, networking and mediation of art and culture
http://blog.tixclub.de – events, festivals, concerts, opera, theater and cinema guide
Eyeout – Mobile art guide App for iPhone download at http://itunes.apple.com/de/app/eyeout-berlin/id373051292?mt=8

GOING OUT

www.restaurantfuehrer-berlin.de
www.berlin030.de
www.berlinatnight.de
www.clubcommission.de

EVENTS

www.berlinonline.de – Comprehensive information about Berlin incl. event calendar
www.berlin-programm.de – well-arranged event calendar
www.zitty.de – Online city magazine
www.tip-berlin.de – Online city magazine
www.blogg.berliner-stadtmagazin.de – Berlin blog

JANUARY TO MARCH

www.fashion-week-berlin.com
www.mercedes-benzfashionweek.com
Fashion Week Fall/Winter takes place in January
www.breadandbutter.com – Bread & Butter – Trade fair for street and urban wear in conjunction with the Fashion Week
www.lange-nacht-der-museen.de – The Long Night of Museums twice a year, at the end of January and the end of August, Berlin's museums are open to the public for one entire night; this night is usually accompanied by various additional cultural events.

www.berlinale.de – In early February; attended by many international movie stars; showing top movies

www.transmediale.de – Transmediale is an international festival for contemporary art and digital culture

www.berlinbiennale.de – Berlin Biennale. Festival of international contemporary art; begins in March every two years

www.gallery-weekend-berlin.de – Gallery weekend during the Berlin Biennale

APRIL TO JUNE

www.karneval-berlin.de – End of May; colorful procession through the streets of Berlin and celebration in the streets in Kreuzberg with participants from over 80 different cultures

http://dmy-berlin.com – DMY Berlin International Design Festival. Takes place beginning of June every year; the festival is the ideal forum for creative professionals and visitors to meet up, catch up or discover the latest trends in direct contact with the international design scene

JULY TO SEPTEMBER

www.fashion-week-berlin.com
www.mercedes-benzfashionweek.com – The Fashion Week Spring/Summer takes place beginning of July

www.breadandbutter.com – Bread & Butter –Trade fair for street and urban wear in conjunction with the Fashion Week

www.lange-nacht-der-museen.de – Second long night of museums of the year takes place in August

www.popkomm.de – One of the world's leading events for music and entertainment in September

OCTOBER TO DECEMBER

www.art-forum-berlin.de – Art Forum Berlin is an international fair and exhibition of contemporary art taking place in October

Cover photo (Kino International)
by Martin Nicholas Kunz

ART

p 10 (Seven Star Gallery), left art "Sharon Tate, Bel-Air" by Peter Brüchmann; middle light installation by Thorsten Heinze; p 11 "Affen Hände, Hamburg" by Frank Wartenberg; all photos courtesy of Seven Star Gallery

p 12 (Me Collectors Room Berlin) photo by Bernd Borchardt; p 13 left art "Equestrian Portrait of King Philip II" 2009, by Kehinde Wiley, photo by Jeurg Iseler; all other photos courtesy of Collectors Room Berlin

p 14, 15 (KW Institute of Contemporary Art) p 14 installation view "No matter How Bright the Light, the Crossing Occurs at Night", 2006; all photos by Martin Nicholas Kunz (further credited as mnk)

p 16, 17 (C/O Berlin) art exhibition "Can you find happiness", 2008, by Bettina Rheims; all photos courtesy of C/O Berlin

p 18-21 (Sammlung Boros) p18 "Colour Sphere", 2006, by Olafur Eliasson, Berlin; p 20 left exterior view of bunker; left middle untitled installation, 2005, by Monika Sosnowska; right construction and installation of tar coated forms in two rooms, 2002, by Santiago Sierra; p 21 "Ventilator", 1997, by Olafur Eliasson; all photos courtesy of Noshe

p 24 (Contemporary Fine Arts Berlin) left art by Tal R, photo by Jan Bauer; middle, middle right + right Katja Strunz, photo by Jan Bauer; p25 by Katja Strunz, photo by Jochen Littkemann; all photos courtesy of Contemporary Fine Arts, Berlin

p 26, 27 (Museum The Kennedys) all photos Museum The Kennedys courtesy of Camera Work

p 28 (Galerie Thomas Schulte) by Juan Uslé, photo by mnk; p 29 middle by Juan Uslé, photo by mnk; middle right, right by Bernhard Martin; photos by mnk, right photo by Lizzy Courage (further credited as lc)

p 30 (Galerie Ulrich Fiedler) p 30 photos by lc, p 31 by mnk

p 32 (East Side Gallery) mural by Peter Lorenz, untitled; p 34 left "Tolerance", by Mary Mackey; middle left, middle, middle right untitled by

Schamil Gimajev; right "Parlo d'Amor", by Ignasi Blanch I Gisbert; p 35 "Danke Andrej Sacharov", by Dimitrij Vrubel; all photos by lc and mnk

p 36 (Berlinische Galerie) blue white plates by Pierre Granoux, mobile by Henrik Schrat, triumphal arc by Miguel Rothschild, white images on back wall by Birgit Maria Wolf, red and black carpet cut-outs in the front by Bernhard Garber; p 38 Fondazione Emilio e Annabianca Vedova, Venezia; left by Ronald de Bloeme; middle by Birgit Maria Wolf; middle right by Ernesto de Fiori; right by Raimund Kummer; all photos by lc and mnk

p 40, 41 (Martin-Gropius-Bau) all photos courtesy of Martin-Gropius-Bau

p 42, 43 (Neue Nationalgalerie) architecture by Ludwig Mies van der Rohe; all photos by lc and mnk

p 44 (Hamburger Bahnhof Museum für Gegenwart Berlin) left, middle, middle right by bpk Bildagentur für Kunst, Kultur und Geschichte, right by mnk; p 45 by mnk

p 46 (Helmut Newton Stiftung im Museum für Fotografie) "Big Nudes" by Helmut Newton, photo by Gerhard Kassner; p 48 exhibition "Helmut Newton FIRED" by Gerhard Kassner; p 49 left exhibition "Helmut Newton SUMO", by Gerhard Kassner; middle, middle right exhibition „Us and Them" by Stefan Müller; right exhibition "Helmut Newton FIRED" by Gerhard Kassner; all photos courtesy of Helmut Newton Stiftung

p 50, 51 (Camera Work) all photos courtesy of Camera Work

p 52 (Haus am Waldsee) by mnk, p 54 left, middle left exhibition „Arturo Herrera - Home" by Arturo Herrera; photo by lc; middle, middle right, right photo by lc; p 55 "Loftcube" by Werner Aisslinger, photo by mnk

ARCHITECTURE

p 60-61 (Aedes am Pfefferberg) all photos by lc and mnk

p 62 (Neues Museum) architecture by David Chipperfield Architects, photo by Jörg von Bruchhausen; p 64 left by Jörg von Bruchhausen; middle, middle right by Ute Zscharnt for David Chipperfield Architects; right by Christian Richters; p 65 by Christian Richters,

CREDITS

all photos courtesy of Stiftung Preußischer Kultur-
besitz/David Chipperfield Architects
p 66, 67 (Jacob-und-Wilhelm-Grimm-Zentrum) architecture by Max Dudler, photos by Stefan Müller;
all photos by Jacob-und-Wilhelm-Grimm-Zentrum
p 68, 69 (Collegium Hungaricum Berlin) architecture by Schweger Associated Architects; all
photos by lc and mnk
p 70, 71 (Deutsches Historisches Museum) architecture by I. M. Pei; all photos by lc and mnk
p 72, 73 (Niederländische Botschaft) architecture
by Rem Koolhaas; all photos by lc and mnk
p 74, 75 (Hochschule für Musik Hanns Eisler,
Neuer Marstall) architecture by Anderhalten
Architekten; all photos by Werner Huthmacher
p 76 (Mini Loft) architecture by Britta Jürgens
and Matthew Griffin, photo by Matthew Griffin;
p 77 photos by lc and mnk
p 78–81 (Band des Bundes), master planning
by Schultes Frank Architekten; p 78, 79 Paul-
Löbe-Haus, architecture by Stephan Braunfels
Architekten BDA and Bundeskanzleramt, by
Schultes Frank Architekten; p 80 left, middle
Bundeskanzleramt, photo by mnk; right and
p 81 left Deutscher Bundestag, rebuilt architects
Foster + Partners, photo by Roland F. Bauer; left
middle, middle, right (Paul-Löbe-Haus) by mnk
p 82, 83 (Akademie der Künste) architecture by
Behnisch & Partner and Werner Durth; left and
right photos by mnk
p 84, 85 (Denkmal für die ermordeten Juden
Europas) architecture by Peter Eisenman; photos
by mnk
p 86 (Science Center Medizintechnik) architecture
by Gnädiger Architekten; photo courtesy of Otto
Bock HealthCare GmbH; p 88 all photos courtesy
of Science Center Medizintechnik
p 90 (E-Werk) architecture by HSH Hoyer Schindele Hirschmüller, left by Anne Krieger, p 91 left,
middle left by HSH Architekten; middle, middle
right by Noshe, right by Anne Krieger; all photos
by HSH Architekten
p 94 (Topographie des Terrors) architecture by
Ursula Wilms and landscape architecture by
Heinz W. Hallmann; photos left, middle left,
middle, middle right by Stefan Josef Müller; right

exterior view by Gerald Freyer; p 95 exterior view
by Gerald Freyer, all photos courtesy of Stiftung
Topographie des Terrors
p 96-99 (Jüdisches Museum Berlin) architecture
by Daniel Libeskind; all photos by lc and mnk
p 100, 101 (Liquidrom) architecture by Meinhard
von Gerkan; all photos by lc and mnk
p 102, 103 (Bauhaus-Archiv Berlin) architecture by
Walter Gropius, Alex Cvijanovic und Hans Bandel;
photos by lc and mnk
p 104–107 (Philologische Bibliothek) architecture
by Foster + Partners; all photos by lc and mnk

p 112, 113 (Ackselhaus & blue home) photos by mnk
p 114, 115 (Soho House Berlin) all photos courtesy of Soho House Berlin
p 116, 117 (Hotel AMANO) photos by lc and mnk
p 118, 119 (Cosmo Hotel Berlin) all photos courtesy of Cosmo Hotel Berlin
p 120–123 (Hotel Michelberger) photos by lc and
mnk
p 126, 127 (Themroc) photos by lc and mnk
p 128, 129 (Oliv) photos by lc and mnk
p 130, 131 (Tadshikische Teestube) photos by
lc and mnk
p 132, 133 (Cha Chà Positive Eating) interior design
by Gunvor Lundgard; photos by lc and mnk
p 134, 135 (Birgit von Heintze Interiors) all photos
courtesy of Birgit von Heintze Interiors
p 136, 137 (Lunettes Selection) photos by lc and
mnk
p 138, 139 (Dandy of the Grotesque) photos by lc
p 140, 141 (Salon Bennett) photos by mnk
p 142, 143 (Schönhauser Design) photos by lc
and mnk
p 144, 145 (Buchhandlung Walther König)
photos by lc and mnk
p 146, 147 (Quartier 206) photos by Quartier 206
p 148, 149 (Exil Wohnmagazin) photos by lc and
mnk
p 150, 151 (Bücherbogen am Savignyplatz)
photos by lc and mnk
p 152, 153 (Villa Harteneck) all photos courtesy
of Villa Harteneck
p 154, 155 (Kino International) photos by mnk

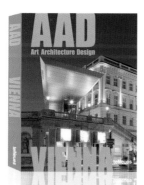

ISBN 978-3-8327-9434-7

ISBN 978-3-8327-9435-4

UPCOMING TITLES
BARCELONA, LONDON + PARIS

© 2010 Idea & concept by Martin Nicholas Kunz, Lizzy Courage Berlin
Selected, edited and produced by Martin Nicholas Kunz, Lizzy Courage Berlin, www.lizzycourage.de
Texts by Raphael Guillou, Gabriele Spengler, Aishah El Muntasser
Editorial coordination: Aishah El Muntasser, Marijana Kelava, Lea Bauer
Copy editing: Arndt Jasper, Sabine Scholz
Art direction: Lizzy Courage Berlin
Imaging and pre-press: printworks Druckdienstleistungen GmbH, mace.Stuttgart
Translations: Übersetzungsbüro RR Communications Romina Russo,
Christie Tam (English), Samantha Michaux (French), Pablo Álvarez (Spanish)

© 2010 teNeues Verlag GmbH + Co. KG, Kempen

teNeues Verlag GmbH + Co. KG
Am Selder 37, 47906 Kempen // Germany
Phone: +49 (0)2152 916-0, Fax: +49 (0)2152 916-111
e-mail: books@teneues.de

Press department // Andrea Rehn
Phone: +49 (0)2152 916-202, e-mail: arehn@teneues.de

teNeues Publishing Company
7 West 18th Street, New York, NY 10011 // USA
Phone: +1 (0)212 627 9090, Fax: +1 (0)212 627 9511

teNeues Publishing UK Ltd.
21 Marlowe Court, Lymer Avenue, London SE19 1LP // Great Britain
Phone: +44 (0)20 8670 7522, Fax: +44 (0)20 8670 7523

teNeues France S.A.R.L.
39, rue des Billets, 18250 Henrichemont // France
Phone: +33 (0)2 48 26 93 48, Fax: +33 (0)1 70 72 34 82

www.teneues.com

While we strive for utmost precision in every detail, we cannot be held responsible
for any inaccuracies, neither for any subsequent loss or damage arising.
Bibliographic information published by the Deutsche Nationalbibliothek.
The Deutsche Nationalbibliothek lists this publication in the Deutsche Nationalbibliografie;
detailed bibliographic data are available in the Internet at http://dnb.d-nb.de.

Printed in the Czech Republic
ISBN: 978-3-8327-9433-0